CW01108644

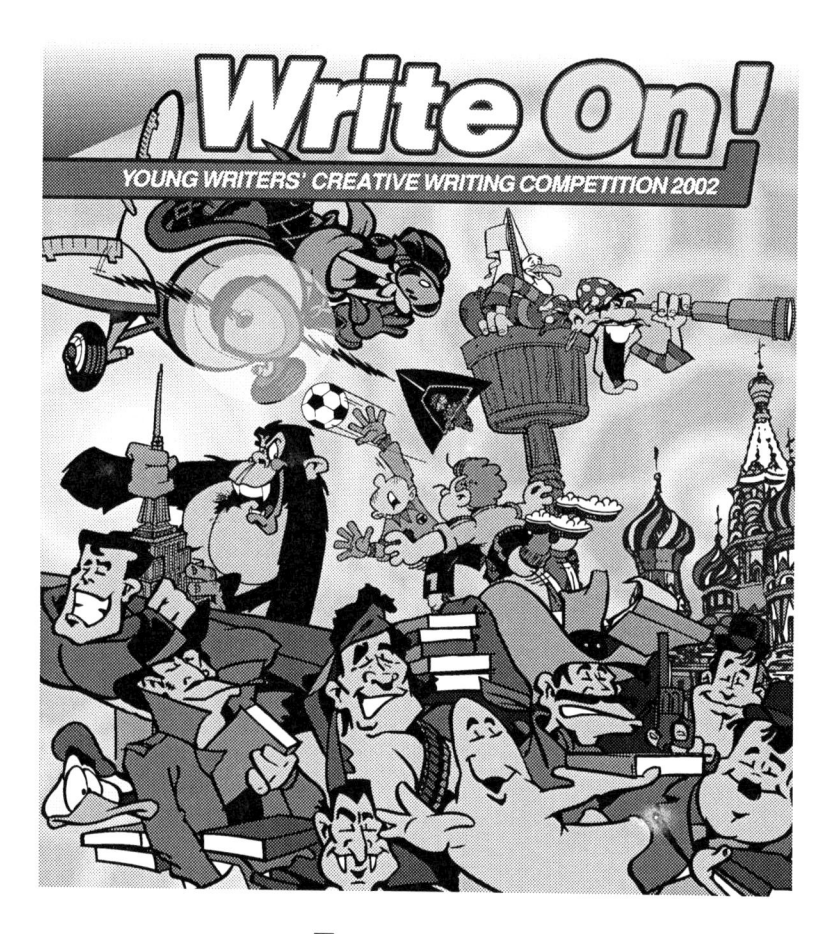

Write On!
YOUNG WRITERS' CREATIVE WRITING COMPETITION 2002

LONDON

Edited by Allison Dowse

First published in Great Britain in 2002 by
YOUNG WRITERS
Remus House,
Coltsfoot Drive,
Peterborough, PE2 9JX
Telephone (01733) 890066

All Rights Reserved

Copyright Contributors 2002

HB ISBN 0 75433 990 4
SB ISBN 0 75433 991 2

FOREWORD

This year, Young Writers proudly presents a showcase of the best short stories and creative writing from today's up-and-coming writers.

We set the challenge of writing for one of our four themes - 'General Short Stories', 'Ghost Stories', 'Tales With A Twist' and 'A Day In The Life Of . . .'. The effort and imagination expressed by each individual writer was more than impressive and made selecting entries an enjoyable, yet demanding, task.

Write On! London is a collection that we feel you are sure to enjoy - featuring the very best young authors of the future. Their hard work and enthusiasm clearly shines within these pages, highlighting the achievement each story represents.

We hope you are as pleased with the final selection as we are and that you will continue to enjoy this special collection for many years to come.

CONTENTS

Barlby Primary School
- Sophian Chhayra — 1
- Sam Cole — 2
- Connor Kinahan — 4
- Karl Thomas-Coyle — 5
- Miriam Serghini — 6
- Maliha Al-Kademi — 8
- Shaheen Rahman — 10
- Elias Mousli — 11
- Simeon Major — 12
- Rosanna White — 13
- Luke West — 14
- Stacey Nugent — 15
- Hanna Castelino — 16
- Katie Sexton — 18
- Kwabena Ahenkorah — 20

Bowes Primary School
- Puja Mehta — 22
- Jordan Gayle — 23
- Lyle Holloway — 24
- Michael Christodoulou — 25
- Jake — 26
- Hakan Sipcauns — 27

Christchurch Bentinck Primary School
- Connor Mills — 28
- Mehma Rahman — 29
- Rhys Barnfather-Jackson — 30
- Leah Aristide — 31
- Charlie Faulkner — 32
- Sean Twomey — 33
- Zain Alhasani — 34
- Sam Chmaissani — 35
- Pensiri Nakan — 36
- Redha Altaie — 38

Helen Yemane	39

Edinburgh Primary School

Zakariya Modan	40
Saira Khan	42
Atia Raja	44
Hannah-Leah Daley	45
Natasha Akram	46
Mahomed Rawat	48
Tatiana N'Dombasi	49
Hamza Kayani	50
Dean Grioli	51
Tauheed Ahmed	52
Melody Masara	54
Hayley Russ	56
Samuel Hoque	57
Farha Sonvadi	58
Jourdane DeCourcy-Nolan	60
Irfana Patel	61
Mehtab Yousaf	62
Muneeba Munawar	63
Hadika Maqsood	64
Nayyar Ali	65
Tanish Chaudry	66
Anisa Fazal	67
Kelly Drury	68
Zuleikha Anwar	69
Yazmin Grioli	70
Mayra Azam	71
Nida Syed	72
Shameelah Siddeeq	73

Falconbrook Primary School

Jordan Gibling	74

Flora Gardens School

James Fell & Mohammed Hussein	75
Sarwar Ali & Amir-Ali Bazazi	76

Ahmed Jumale & Karl de St Aubin	78
Nataleigh Taylor & Romina Fatemi	79
Abida Rahimi & Jamie Joahill	80
Bashira Meah & Natalie Pearson	82
Maryam Zarif, Masuma Ahmed & Lena Samirie	83
Aicha Jaowad, Sophie Stanley & Katie Pemberton	84
Pida Ahmed & Myran Maughan-Dineen	86

Glenbrook Junior School

Chituru Osumah	88
Christopher Cole	90
Tyrone Huggins	92
Rea Nwigwe	94
Anthony Street	95
Kemi Olukoga	96
Sanna Khan	97
Brian Blackwood	98
Joanne Wallace	100
Aisha Green	101
Niyonu Agana-Burke	102
Kristina Madden	104
Calvin Johnson	107
Denton De Frietas	108
Kori Hendrickson	109
Luke Bradbury	110
Mabina Beccari	111
Daisy San	112
Elizabeth Muir	114
Tayo Oke	116
Mark Buchanan	117
Akin Anderson	118
Samson Abayomi	119
Nana Frimpong	120
Nicholas Marongwe	121
Ayo Unoarumhi	122

Grange Park Prep School
    Natasha Sheppard   124
    Leanne Kean   125
    Victoria Ware   126
    Emily Ross   127
    Lydia Mills   128

Guardian Angels RC JMI School
    Rosie Inns   129

Hampstead Hill Pre-Prep School
    Oliver Wilkinson   130
    William Snell-Mendoza   131
    Milton Karamani   132
    Sebastian Gemes   133
    Tom Wilkinson   134
    Archie Wells   135
    Jack Mead   136
    Daniel Walsh   137

Larkswood Junior School
    James Welsh   138
    Calum Doyle   139
    Charlotte Bacuzzi   140
    JJ Haynes   141
    Emma Moorhouse   142
    Katie Morris   143
    Emma Mahoney   144
    Ben Thompson   145
    Jamie Flory   146
    Eileen Kealey   148
    Mitchell Williams   149

Lathom Junior School
    Janani Paramsorthy   150
    Samreen Iftikhar   151
    Jimena Meza Mitcher   152
    Amira Lounis   154

Juwan Sivathas	155
North Bridge House School	
Ritika Daswani	156
Simon Arden	157
Natalie Mallin	158
Seth Elton	159
Olga Formalnova	160
Juliet McNelly	161
Jonathan Fernandes	162
St Agnes RC Primary School, Barnet	
Conor O'Sullivan	163
Megan Abbott	164
St Scholastica's RC Primary School, Hackney	
Perry Tobin-Stevens	165
Ben Slade	166
Dana McCusker	167
Kevin Kotey	168
Jean-Claude Isaie	169
Hannah Phillips	170
Jade Smith	171
Charlotte Dunne	172
Franklyn Addo Koroma	173
Toby Osei-Baffour	174
Euan McIntyre	175
St Stephen's CE Primary School	
Jacob Crofts	176
Maysun Hoque	177
Dysney Cline-Decker	178
Yasmin Abdi	179
Stroud Green Primary School	
Rachel Koramoah	180
Denisha Koramoah	181
Chinyere Nwimo Ogu	182

Summerside Primary School
   Aliya Fenghour   184

William Davies Primary School
   Naeem Mitha   185
   Asma Patel   186
   Nabilah Sannan   187
   Neelam Samplay   188
   Pooja Bharucha   190
   Salma Zannath   192

William Patten Primary School
   Archie Backhouse & Zed Callaghan   194
   Jethro Jenkins   196
   Eleanor Sluman & Nat Smith   198
   Oliver Ings-Williams & Harvey Pegg   200

The Stories

FORGETFUL ALEX

'Alex, have you woken up yet?' shouted Mum.
'I'll be down in a minute,' replied Alex.

As usual Alex and his friend went to school together when all of a sudden, Alex remembered something but he didn't know what it was.
At play time Alex met his sister, Emma.
'Alex do you remember what day it is today?' said Emma.
'Yes I do, it's a school day,' replied Alex.
'No it isn't, it's Mum's birthday, you have nearly forgotten it every year,' argued Emma.
'Have you got Mum a present yet?' she asked.
'No, I'll get her one after school.' answered Alex.
'You're probably going to forget that too,' laughed Emma.

After school, Alex went to the flower shop, but you wouldn't believe it, it was closed and there was only one more flower shop left, next to his house and according to his watch it was closing in five minutes. So he went running and luckily he got there just in time but the other problem was that the party might have already started.

When he arrived at home, luckily the party hadn't started. His mum was glad because he got her a present *this time.*

Sophian Chhayra (11)
Barlby Primary School

ENGLAND'S CUP

The big match today for England. It's England Vs Sweden. I think it's going to be a good match today in Japan. The formation is 3-5-2 for England. In goal for England is David Seaman, at the back is Gareth Southgate, Sol Campbell, Rio Ferninand and in midfield is Owen Hargreaves, David Beckham, Paul Scholes, Kieran Dyer, Ashley Cole. Up front are Teddy and Owen. Kick-off and England are already on the run. *Goal!* Owen has scored for England. First half has gone now. It's the second half now and still 1-0 to England and it's over for Sweden on their first game.

It's England's second game against Nigeria and they are a good team, but England can draw and win the next game to get through. It's the same team that played against Sweden. Kick-off! England are on the ball and is it going to be a goal? No! They fouled Owen and it's a free kick! Beckham is taking it. He shoots, that's a *goal!* It's 1-0 to England. And half-time has gone. It's the second half and England are on the ball and Teddy shoots. *Goal!* There's one minute to go. The match has finished. England are top in their group!

It is the hardest game in the group. It's England Vs Argentina. Kick-off has started and Argentina are on the ball. Veron shoots . . . *goal!* What a superb goal from Veron! It is 1-0 to Argentina and the first half is over. As the second half begins Crespo takes a shot and it just goes over the bar. There are two minutes to go in the second-half and Michael Owen is on the ball. He is one on one with the keeper. He goes around him and he shoots . . . *Goal!* And it is 1-1. We are through.

It's the quarter finals and it's England Vs Belgium. Kick off has started and David Beckham is on the ball, he takes a shot. *Goal!* The first-half has gone and it's 1-0 to England. The second half has begun and Joe Cole has shot. *Goal!* What a goal by the young Cole. That was a late winner, and England has finished. England are in the finals because Brazil are out because they were beating up the Japan fans.

England are in the finals against France. England are playing their best squad. Kick-off has started and France are on the ball. They shoot. That's a *goal* by Henry! France are on the ball again. They shoot. That's a *goal* by Zidane. The first half has finished. Second half has begun.

And England are on the ball, they shoot. That's a *goal* by Owen. England are on the ball again. They shoot. It's a *goal* by Gerrard. We're in the last seconds and it's a free kick to England. Beckham takes it. The ball is flying in the air, it goes in the back of the net. *Goal!* England has won the FIFA World Cup! David Beckham picks up the cup. England are the champions!

Sam Cole (11)
Barlby Primary School

SPOOK STORIES

Bang!
'What was that?' said Billy.
'Oh that was nothing,' said Sophian, trying to put a pole in the back of the truck. Then they went on their camping trip. When they got there they found where they wanted to camp and set up. When it got dark they read some books, then Billy started to read something out loud.

'One night two kids were in their tent in the forest and they were killed by a wolf. When the rescue people came, all they found was the wolf and its bloody mouth.'

When it got dark they go into their tent and fell asleep. They were awoken by the sound of a wolf. They both managed to get the words *wolf* out of their mouths - they were frightened to their bones. Then they heard a rip in the tent. They both backed up as far as they could go, then they saw a black figure walking into the tent and they screamed. When they saw the wolf's white teeth their screams echoed through the night.
'Billy, would you stop reading please!'

Connor Kinahan (11)
Barlby Primary School

SHORT STORY

They raced down the slopes, hitting each other any way possible. Cid is in front, not Zell. Over a jump. Spectacular tricks. Another jump. Neither of them going very high, it's still neck and neck, anybody's race. And the other four competitors are way behind these two superb snowboarders.

'You can't beat me,' says Cid confidently.

'Yes I can,' replies Zell. 'you're the one that can't beat me.'

They're nearing the finish line, they both jump to do a trick . . . Cid falls and tumbles, Zell stops before the finish line. He's just showing off. Now he's crossed the line.

'I'm the champion you can never beat me,' says Zell.

'I knew I should have chosen a different character. Can we play *Final Fantasy Ten* now or *Breath of Fire Four?*' says Cid, trying to persuade his friend.

'If you win you can choose.' Zell giggles a bit, as he says it, because he knows he will always win.

'But I will never win because you're too good and I'm not,' Cid says dully, feeling bored.

'Then that is a real big pity, you will just have to keep trying your hardest then.'

Karl Thomas-Coyle (11)
Barlby Primary School

THE BAD NEWS

'I'm having a baby,' Mum shouted. 'but not right now.'

Miriam and Dad sprinted down the stairs, across the corridor and rushed straight into the kitchen.
'Did you say what I thought you said?' asked Miriam, trying to get her breath back.
'How could this happen?' whispered Dad.
Mum looked strangely at Miriam, she wanted to tell her something but she thought it could wait until tomorrow.

Five, four, three, two, one, *ring, ring* went the alarm clock. Miriam struggled to get up, like always, but when she got up Mum was standing right beside her bed.
'Honey, I need to ask you something but you don't have to answer right away. You know a baby's coming and it needs a bedroom, so I thought it could have Ben's room,' Mum suggested.
'How could you even think about it? Ben's my brother and he's dead,' Miriam said, with tears falling down her eyes. Then she ran out of her bedroom and locked herself inside the bathroom. Then a few days after, Miriam said yes.

Straight after that day, Miriam and Mum started pulling the wallpaper off and putting up beautiful yellow ducks with lovely hearts above. Mum was of course, faster than Miriam but then she stumbled across a door which was hidden behind the wallpaper.
'Cool door, let's go inside' said Miriam.
'No! I mean we need to finish off this and go to sleep so we have no time to go in,' replied Mum.

After the door thing happened, Miriam told all her friends about it, (wouldn't you?) but when she told them they thought she was joking.
'It might be nothing,' said one of Miriam's friends.

Miriam and a few of her friends were standing right in front of the door. Miriam opened the door and stepped in. Her friends stepped in. The door *slammed shut*. They walked down what seemed to be a corridor.

She looked to the left and saw dirty and musty bones, mostly skulls. She looked to the right and saw nothing, not even a scratch. She saw a huge coffin in front of her. She took two deep breaths and with all her might she opened it.

'*Brother,*' said Miriam . . .

Miriam Serghini (11)
Barlby Primary School

SHORT STORY

'Wake up Harry!' shouted Harry's mum as loud as she could.
Harry was too tired to even answer. Then suddenly, as he saw the time on his watch, he then immediately scrambled out of bed and started to shout. 'Mum! Why didn't you wake me up earlier?' Harry said as he screamed his head off.
'Stop screaming! You'll wake up the neighbours, or even crack the windows!' Harry's mum started to laugh.

The next moment Harry put his clothes on as fast as he could, so quick that he forgot to do up his buttons. Then he ran to the train station with an angry face.

As he went in he saw a very long queue for the tickets. 'Oh no!' said Harry to himself. The queue followed on outside. He waited and waited, which felt like years passing by. Finally it was Harry's turn. He was fifteen minutes late. He was in *big* trouble. Then he rushed down the electric stairs. It was getting late and the train was getting late too. He waited and heard a train coming. He crossed his fingers and then he realised that it was his train.

He was the first person to get on the train. It felt like a hundred years until Harry got off the train. He ran as fast as a cheetah. It was pouring with rain.

Harry rushed into the school office. 'Can I . . . I . . . see Miss Ray?' stuttered Harry.
'Yes you can, go in,' said Mrs Tim. Harry took a deep breath and went in.
'Hello Harry!' Miss Ray said joyfully.
'I'm l . . . a . . . te for scho . . . ol.' Harry was trying really hard to get his words out properly.
'What? I'll have to write a letter home! Go back to class,' shouted Miss Ray.

He had a really miserable day. He usually got all the answers right, but this time he didn't.

It was home-time and he went to collect his letter from the office. Harry gave his letter to his mum. He was left knowing what was written in his letter.

Maliha Al-Kademi (11)
Barlby Primary School

FORGETFUL ME

I couldn't believe it, it was the worst day of my life, it was terrible, unbelievable ah . . . and horrible. This is how it goes.

It was Saturday, 6th November 1999. I love Saturday, no school.
'Get up John, go to school, you're late!' shouted Mum.
'It's Saturday,' I said shakily.
'You forgot again.'

As I put my school uniform on I thought, urgh. I put my other clothes on, went downstairs and never saw Mum. I made my way to school. As I got in, there was a big roar at me.
'You're late!' bellowed the teacher.
'But, but . . . Miss Cabberages,' I said.
'Don't *'but me'* son. No homework or uniform, go to the head teacher.'
I made my way there. 'I'm in trouble,' I said.
'I thought so, no uniform, late and no homework. Also where's my pencil?'
'I thought it was mine, so I snapped it in half,' I put a big smile on my face.
'Take that smile off your face and get your group here.'

In the end it was bad but my forgetfulness is getting worse.

Shaheen Rahman (11)
Barlby Primary School

FLYING TIME

Sam had just gone to the bathroom after feeding Tommy at 17:00.
'You stay here Tommy and don't get out of your pram, don't you even dare. As soon s I come out I do *not*, I repeat, I do not want to see a mess as usual.'
But Tommy took no notice and just repeated everything that he said.
'God, *who* does he think he is?' Tommy questioned.

17:05
As soon as Sam got out of the bathroom, he turned around. *'Huh!'* he shouted. He turned back around, wiped his eyes and whispered, 'Oh no!' He turned around one last time and couldn't believe his eyes, hewiped them once again, then . . . he exploded. *'What have you done to the wall. It's, it's so ugly I can't even spit the words out.'*

Sam kept his cool, he had to go through five large, long, twisted years.
'It's pink, mouldy green and yellow, It's so bright that it almost blinded me. If Mum sees this dreadful, messy paint on the wall, she will be devastated!' screamed Sam.

17:30
'I've got no time to lose,' Sam said strictly.
Zoom, he got the cloth, snatch and the bucket. He started cleaning, he closed his eyes, wiped once and the wall was as good as new.

18:00
5, 4, 3, 2, 1, done it.
Ding-dong,
'Honey, it's me. Oh I've forgot the milk,' Mum panicked.
'Sam, honey, I'll come back in a minute,' Mum suggested.
Bang! Sam fainted.

Elias Mousli (10)
Barlby Primary School

I Know What You Did Last Summer

It was one October night when there was a full moon. There lived a family called the Clumps. They were making a lovely roast dinner for the children, Mum, Dad and Nan.

'Mum, pass me the salad please.'
'Come on Dad you're not doing anything,' Mum gasped to Dad as usual.
'I've got a headache that's why I'm not doing anything. What do you expect me to do?' Dad moaned.
'Go upstairs and rest off your headache dear,' Nan replied.

Dad went upstairs and opened the door . . .
When he opened the door he found the window opening and closing and there was some writing on the curtain, saying *I know what you did last summer* in red writing. Dad ran downstairs with fear.

'What's wrong Honey?' Mum said in a squeaky voice.
'Upstairs,' Dad said breathlessly.
'I will go up,' she said in a brave voice.

Mum went upstairs.
'It's fabulous. Nice cushions, beds, even the room is scrubbed.'
Dad saw somebody with a black cloak and a hook. He rain downstairs.
'Ahhh.'
Mum ran downstairs and found Dad on the stairs losing blood. Nan came and fainted. Mum could hear the kids saying faintly,
'Help,' Mum ran into the front room and opened the door. Suddenly the lights started to go on and off. The children were crying.
'Help Mum, help we're going to die.'
'Just stay there Honey, I'm coming.'
Mum ran across and got the children then ran to Dad.
Dad was gone.
'Children we are leaving,' said Mum.
(Every person who lived there always got haunted.)

Simeon Major (11)
Barlby Primary School

SHORT STORY

During football training, a boy with big ears and an Afro was practising scoring a goal but he couldn't kick the ball. After an hour he was still trying to kick the ball but still couldn't.

After football, all the others called him Afro Man and Big Ears because he didn't have a go at kicking the ball.

When he got home he tried kicking the ball against the wall in his garden but he still couldn't kick the ball. Then he started daydreaming. He dreamed he was the best footballer in the world and scored a lot of goals. While he was daydreaming, he kicked the ball for the first time in his entire life and broke a window!

The next morning there was a note left on the table that read;

> *I'm going to get you a football kit and you're going to get a haircut whether you like it or not. It makes your ears look big and it looks silly.*
> Dad

When they got the kit and the haircut, it was time for football training. Suddenly, he became the best football player. Then he was chosen for the championship.

The final match was the time when he was there without his kit and a friend loaned him one. When it was nearly the end of the match, he kicked the ball, hoping it would go in and it did.
Goal!
The match was over, they won.

Rosanna White (11)
Barlby Primary School

GHOST STORY

Every night a group of people would always go down to the forest and tell stories.

One night the group went to the forest and started to tell their stories. The leader threw dust into the fire and started to tell the story, *The Ghost In the Darkness*.

One day a boy, Simon, was walking around the creepiest part of the neighbourhood on Hallowe'en. Only two hours to go till *you know who* is set to reappear. Nobody ever spoke of his name because they feared he might come back. But one night Simon spoke it. From out of nowhere the monster appeared. Sitting on his pale, white horse was Nearly Headless Nick, chuckling to himself.

A few days later, Simon found out where Nearly Headless Nick lived, which was the forest. So he walked to the bridge then crossed it and waited for the horseman to come and just then a galloping sound echoed through the forest and Simon had to run. Nearly Headless Nick had vanished.

Luke West (11)
Barlby Primary School

DON'T BE SCARED

'I'm so happy you won this prize Honey. We can put it up right here in the living room so everyone can see it.'
'Mum! Why? Why in the front room? Why not somewhere no one can see it?' moaned Matthew to his mum, embarrassed.
'No and no buts! Oh and put that tongue back in your mouth!' Matthew's mum said crossly outside the room.

That night, Matthew slept downstairs in his tent, thinking about the book award he had won earlier that day at school for having the best story in class. When his little friend Lisa (the ghost) showed up, Matthew ran out of the tent as fast as his legs would carry him. She was behind him. Then for the rest of that night Matthew sat up in the middle of the cold front room. The next day he went to see the doctor.

'Doctor I need some *help!* I keep seeing a ghost. One in particular, Lisa. What should I do?' Matthew asked.
In return he got, 'Are you feeling OK?'

Matthew could tell he wasn't getting any help. That night he slept in his own bed. When he closed his eyes he saw a ghost. He opened his eyes and the ghost was still there. He screamed, she stayed. Matthew was confused; the ghost put her hand out, so did he. They shook hands and were not scared of one another anymore.

Stacey Nugent (11)
Barlby Primary School

SHORT STORY

In the hot, untidy, getting dirtier every day room, Teepo was getting more bored by the minute. He had nothing to do. The electricity was running low, so they had to save up and all his games he had completed. So he could either do homework or housework.

'Aw man! Homework or cleaning!' As he said this, a voice came from the background.
'Why don't you do the cleaning for once?'
'What? Oh all right!' he said, thinking he had done it before.

As Teepo got up, he slowly made his way to the bathroom like it was the gates of Hell. When he was half-way through cleaning, he stupidly jumped in the bath, hoping to make it more fun, but this foolish act only made him dirty. Then suddenly he got sucked into the plughole. Teepo tried to scream but nothing came out, at least not until he was stuck down there.

As Teepo got down, he started to wander around, trying to get an idea of where he was. 'It all happened so quickly. I . . . I ho . . . hope I hit my head and am now asleep.' But alas he was not; instead he was in the filthy pipes running through his house.

When he finally realised where he was, he started to think about all the foul creatures that could live there. 'There could be pieces of filth that feed on hu . . .' Before Teepo could finish his sentence he got interrupted.
'He, he, he. There isn't anything like *that!*' laughed a high, squeaky voice.
'W . . .who are you?'
'Look in front of you.'
'I only see a dead spider!'
'Hey! I'm not dead!' declared the spider, opening its purple eyes.
'How can you talk?'
'Spiders are smarter than you think! Now let's get down to business. We both want to get out, right? Now how do we get out?'

After a little while they came up with a brilliant idea! Teepo grabbed some of the spider's silk and threw it so it got hooked onto something. Then he climbed on the spider and they climbed out. Then Teepo picked up the spider and put him in a drawer where he would be safe.

Hanna Castelino (11)
Barlby Primary School

GRANNY'S HERE

You might be wondering why I am packing, well let me tell you why. We're moving, (we've moved so many times before I have lost count). We are moving because Dad has got a new job. Anyway, apart from moaning about it, I am a bit excited because Dad says the house is big! I have never lived in a big house before! (I've only ever lived in a small house).
'Come on,' shouted Mum.
'Coming,' I replied.
As we all got in the car I said goodbye to the house. After many boring hours . . .
'Finally,' I said with a sigh of relief, 'we're here!'
'Come on,' said Dad, 'let's go in.'

Do you know, the house was quite big as well. We all walked in (wow! I thought to myself, this house is huge).

While Mum was doing the dinner I was looking around my new bedroom (I had a bit of trouble finding it at first).

After dinner I went to bed. As I pulled the covers over my legs, I heard something. It wasn't actually something, it was . . . someone. As I lay there the voice kept repeating the same thing over and over again.
'Help me,' it said. By this time I was so scared I couldn't even help myself. I yanked the covers over my head. I wish we'd never moved. A cool bit of air came into the room. By this time I was so scared I let out a big scream. 'Help!' I shouted at the top of my voice. 'Help!'
Mum and Dad walked in. 'What's wrong?' they asked.
'There's something by the window,' I replied.
'Come on you can sleep downstairs.'
I went downstairs.

8:15am Saturday morning (no school thank God) I was lying down watching CD:UK and guess what song was playing - Gareth Gates. I wish he wouldn't be a number one. Mum walked in.

'Come on,' she said in a happy voice. (Mum is never happy she must have got out of the wrong side of the bed.) I got ready and headed for Sainsbury's.
'Chips or burgers?' Mum asked. I hate it when she does this. After ten years of thinking she said chips. We went to queue.
'£19.56 please,' said the woman at the till. After that we left.

'Home at last,' I said as I put the shopping down.

A few months later, while I was laying down on my bed, I saw a really faint shadow (now I am not going through what I went through before). As the shadow began to get clearer, I saw an old woman, she looked like my nan. Actually it was my nan.
'Nan,' I said with a tear of happiness coming down my face. As I sat there talking to her, Mum called me.
'Tim I have something to tell you.'
'What?' I said.
'We are moving.'
I ran upstairs. Nan was not there. While I started packing once again I said my last goodbyes. No matter how many times I have moved, I will always love this house most.

Katie Sexton (11)
Barlby Primary School

THE DISORGANISED HAUNTED PRANK

It was the Monday night that Mark and John were having two friends over for the night. It came 7 o'clock and the guests arrived.

'Whazzzap?' asked Henry, sending a guttering look to Mum's face.
'Nothing just chilling, killing watching TV,' replied Mark trying to impress his friends.
'Come on Scary Movie is about to start,' said John in a rush.

Scary Movie had finished so the children were going to move into the bedroom.

'Who wants to play the dare game?' asked Steven loudly.
'Yeahhh!' all the boys shouted together.
'Boys keep the noise down, you will wake the baby,' shouted Mum in a high tone.
'I double dare you John and Mark to go and scare your mum and make her scream.'

John and Mark set off downstairs to scare their mother, but they did not know that Mum was going to play a little trick on them.

'Crrrrr' the stairs went as the boys went down one by one.

Meanwhile, upstairs Henry and Steven were planning a trick.
'Wait until they get hold of this prank,' Steven said evilly, laughing at Mark.

Downstairs Mum and the two boys were close to each other. The next thing they knew . . .

'Ahhh,' they screamed.
'Mum what are you doing here?' the boys asked.
'Oh nothing just checking around the house.'

In the bedroom Steven and Mark were almost finished with their prank. Time was flying so the boys went down the stairs to complete their prank.

'We are close so be quiet Mark,' Said Steven.
'1, 2, 3, roar!' the boys shouted.
'Ahhhh!' Mum and the other two boys shouted.
'Well let's all say this was one disorganised prank,' Mum said.
'Yea . . .' they said when they were interrupted.
'Aaaawwwoooo!'
'Ahhhh!' they all screamed.

Kwabena Ahenkorah (10)
Barlby Primary School

CRAZY ELEANOR

One rainy wet evening Miss Cumberbatch was working late in 3MC. She was marking the mock SATs they had done that day. She was shivering like mad because it was in the middle of winter.

Suddenly the door opened.
'Who's there?' she whispered nervously, creeping up to the door.
'Oh sorry, I didn't scare you did I?' gasped Miss Honny.
'No, no, no, no you didn't. What are you doing still in school?'
'Oh just marking the mock SATs.' Miss Honny went away.

Then Miss Cumberbatch felt something in the room with her, she carried on.

Suddenly the fan turned on. Miss Cumberbatch ran to the fan and switched it off straight away. Then she felt something sweep past her. Miss Cumberbatch *screamed*.

Miss Honny came racing in.
'I . . . I . . . I just felt something sweep across my back.'
'Oh, that's crazy Eleanor.'
'Who?'

Puja Mehta (8)
Bowes Primary School

JORDAN

Jo and Jordan are twin brothers. They are eleven years old. Jo and Jordan live in Brazil. It is spring 1939. It is the witching hour. It is hot and humid and Lee is the ghost. He is a poltergeist. The last house he was in was in China. They scared him away.

Jordan Gayle (8)
Bowes Primary School

THE THIRSTY GHOST

Lyle and his friend Ishmael were petrified because something was banging on the door. Then their friend Jessie came in and shut the door.

'Evil spirits are banging on the door!' she exclaimed.
'Yikes!' shouted Lyle.

Suddenly the ghost came in the wall and said, 'Give me a drink!'

Lyle Holloway (7)
Bowes Primary School

THE GHOST OF HORROR

One stormy night Mike and Judy were camping. Mike had his own tent. Mike went in his BMW car and listened to some music with his subwoofers in the back. He saw something white in the forest, he called Judy to pack up quickly and she did and quickly jumped in the car and the ghost chopped down a tree.

They were trapped. Mike got his air gun and shot a tree that squashed the ghost. Then he shot the tree that trapped them and crushed through with their car. Then the ghost chucked a sharp knife and stabbed Judy. Mike went 900 mph to the hospital and took her in.
He said, 'She got stabbed.'
Judy had to have an operation.

Michael Christodoulou
Bowes Primary School

REAL GHOST STORY

Once Jake, Pule and Oliver were riding on the road. They went past Jake's old house and the ghosts started to throw things at them. They started to throw things back.

Oliver said, 'Help!' but no one heard him.

Oliver picked up the heaviest thing around him and threw it at the ghost.

Suddenly it all stopped and everything was quiet and Jake, Pule and Oliver rode off.

Jake
Bowes Primary School

DENTIS THE GHOST

Once upon a time someone called Joseph was walking in the woods. It was night-time and there was a fun fair but it was closed.

It was ten o'clock and it was so dark.
'Raa, raa, raa,' Joseph heard a horse at his back, he turned round and saw a ghost.
He said, 'Argh!'
Everyone jumped out of their beds and they saw the ghost as well.

Dentis ate everyone in the world, there was just Joseph left. We went to the ghost and he saw a jacket on the ghost. He tried to take the jacket off but he could not take it off because it was a real ghost. Joseph got the knife and he went to the ghost and killed the ghost and everyone was alive again and they had a party!

Hakan Sipcauns
Bowes Primary School

SAVING THE ANIMALS

One day there was a mermaid. I found the mermaid and it was the best thing of my life. I was amazed when suddenly she gave me a special potion that made me speak to beautiful animals.

The mermaid said, 'Do you want to come to the other side of the world?'
'Yes please.'
'The other side of the world looks like space.'

I decided to save the deep blue sea and the wildlife and also flying animals and the world is always safe, this is how I saved the animals.

I gave them more food and because I could speak to animals I gave them some potion. The mermaid helped me save the animals as well and when we got out of the dazzling sea we looked like human beings again and more mermaids came into the sparkling sea. We even saved space. When I saved space all of the sea went calm.

Connor Mills (8)
Christchurch Bentinck Primary School

UNTITLED

One sunny day Mehma, Monawara and Ayah were going to New York. When they were on the plane it crashed. Everyone had to jump. Everyone saw a little cottage but Mehma, Monawara and Ayah went into an enormous green jungle! They thought no one was in the green jungle, but when they turned around they saw one blue and black tiger and a black and white cheetah.

Mehma, Monawara and Ayah were shocked when they saw the tiger and the cheetah and started running. When they got to the end of the jungle they saw a little cottage. When they went inside they saw everyone that was in the plane.

Mehma Rahman (9)
Christchurch Bentinck Primary School

MY ADVENTURE STORY

Once there were two boys called Rhys and Islam. They were on an important secret mission to destroy a monster. They found a giant hole and they crept towards it. Then they heard stamping and crashing. There it was, the monster they were looking for. It was the biggest monster they had ever seen, it was giant.

Then he said in a giant voice, 'Bye, I'm going to take over the whole world!' They went after him but he hid in Spain and poisoned everyone.

Then the monster went to Australia and this time he bombed them. Then he went to America and shot them. Then to all the other countries, but all of the people came alive again because they found him and got the potion and unpoisoned everyone, then Hasslebaink came and kicked his eyes out and they put him in some lava so everyone was safe forever.

Rhys Barnfather-Jackson (8)
Christchurch Bentinck Primary School

I WENT TO MARS

I went to mars and I saw an ugly alien.

He said, 'I am going to eat you up.' Then the lights went off.

I was really, really scared and when the light came on I sank into the chocolate floor. I soon realised that a mother alien lived there. The mother alien tries to eat people who get stuck in the chocolate in the chocolateon Mars. I was dreaming and when I came up I was really scared. I came in a fast rocket and I was eating all the chocolate from Mars. I saw aliens when I was looking around Mars. I got out because the mother alien lifted me up, the other aliens saw my head coming out of the chocolate floor and the other aliens pulled my head out, then I went back in my fast rocket.

Leah Aristide
Christchurch Bentinck Primary School

MY ADVENTURE STORY

You will never believe what happened to me and my friend when we went to the park. Me and my friend were playing hide and seek. Leah counted and I hid.

I was hiding when suddenly a wolf came to get me. Then the wolf took me to his cave and locked me in.

I tried to get out by the gate but it was locked. The wolf came back in and tried to eat me, so I kicked him and he stopped biting and fell asleep.

When he awoke and tried to eat me again. I tried talking to him. I told him not to hurt me and he said, 'OK, I won't eat you but will you not kick me again?' Then we were friends.

Charlie Faulkner
Christchurch Bentinck Primary School

DANGER AROUND THE PLANET

Sean was on a mission. One day he landed on an unknown planet.

Suddenly an alien appeared out of nowhere. He started shooting and so did Sean. He was moving backwards then he fell into a hole. He saw a great ball of energy. He touched the great ball of energy. Suddenly it got very hot. Then he used his rocket booster to get out of the place but the alien shot him out of the sky. He saw an alien gun, picked it up and shot at the alien. The alien fell asleep and stopped shooting. Sean put him in his rocket and flew away from the planet. He put the alien on another planet.

Sean Twomey
Christchurch Bentinck Primary School

THE EVIL FORCE

Once there was an evil force that completed its plan to destroy the world. But in the world the security activated the world's shield. Anyway, me, my cousin and brother were playing *Grand Theft Auto Three*.

We had almost completed the last level, but then we died. We couldn't be bothered to do it again, so we switched of the PS2. Then we went to watch TV.

Then the evil force did a blast at the Earth, just before we switched on the TV. The shield affected the blast.

Then the evil force did it until the shield wore out. The security activated the shield again. The evil force did it again at its full power. The shield affected it. The blast hit the evil force and destroyed him.

Zain Alhasani
Christchurch Bentinck Primary School

DAVID BECKHAM, STEVEN AND I GO TO MARS

One day I went to Mars with David Beckham and Steven. I was shocked when I saw a large Smarties chocolate castle. We went inside the tall castle and got lost among all the Mars bar wrappers which made a wall. We couldn't find our way out. Suddenly . . . we heard a loud bang. I looked outside the window and saw an alien shooting the castle with his astonishing laser.

We had to get the alien to stop shooting us. We rushed to a window. David Beckham went first, I went next and Steven was last to jump out of the window. We landed on some soft chocolate. We saw what the alien was doing, he was . . . shrinking.

We made up a plan.
'We have to let him shrink,' I said.
He was about thirty centimetres when we finished our plan. We threw the alien into a chocolate pool. He tried to get out but the pool was too strong. We made the castle nicer and cleaner and also brighter. We went home in our super, gigantic rocket. We decided never to go there again.

Sam Chmaissani (8)
Christchurch Bentinck Primary School

MY ADVENTURE STORY

Once upon a time, in a very rich house, lived a girl called Betty. One day Betty said to Alice, 'Let's go on an adventure.'
Alice said, 'No way.'
But Betty said, 'Let's go to a spooky mystery maze underground in a fantastic island where all the animals lived a long time ago.'
Alice said, 'OK.'
So the two girls went on their journey. Then they made it and Betty said, 'There's the hole.'

They went inside the hole and Alice said, 'Look at the dead people and the Queen of Hearts' army.'
Then one of the soldiers caught Alice and threw her into an unlocked secret maze with crocodiles everywhere.
Betty said, 'I have to speak with someone who can help Alice.'
Then the Queen came and said, 'No one will throw me into the crocodile pool.'

Then Betty found the Queen cackling with laughter and said, 'Give me back my friend.'
And the Queen said, 'No way.'
Betty said, 'Why not?'
'Because first you must go inside and unlock a secret maze so you can get your friend back.'
Betty said, 'It's a deal. I will come back tomorrow evening.

The next morning came and Betty went to the Queen's palace and said, 'Now Queen, take me to a secret maze.'
The Queen said, 'Your command.'
Betty said to herself, maybe she gave me a trick, but then she heard Alice crying, 'Help me'
Betty was walking and heard the Queen say, 'I gave the girl a trick.'

Betty felt strong and she wanted to be Queen and said, 'I am going to throw you into the crocodile pool.'
So she threw her in and she was gone. Betty rushed to save Alice and she found the key. Then she saw the door and opened it. They went safely home and lived happily ever after.

Pensiri Nakan (7)
Christchurch Bentinck Primary School

THE HEADLESS MAN

One day my friends, Sam and Connor and I went on a trip on a boat. On the way the boat went off track. We were lost so we went to the next island, it had a big skull. There were jangling sounds. The skull smelt bad.

We looked around. Sam, Connor and I went in and we saw . . . a man with no head. He chased us. I saved Sam but I got caught by the man who was going to drop me into a shark pool. I was saved by a boat with David Beckham in it.
He said, 'Good thing I saw you.'
We had no idea what would happen next. We were not safe.

Redha Altaie (8)
Christchurch Bentinck Primary School

THE BOYS WHO TRAVELLED TO A DESERT IN A HOT AIR BALLOON

One exciting day in a hot air balloon, there were four people called Kevin, Luke, Rhys and Steve. They were travelling to a burning desert.

When they landed, they had a drink but it was very quick. When they had it they started to dig for crystals. They dug for crystals because they thought they would become rich. They loved to travel but didn't like to waste time. They collected so many that they didn't keep them all. They travelled back to Spain where they were in the first place.

They travelled back with the hot air balloon.

When they landed they sold crystals. One woman always came and saw them and bought them. She gave them a huge white house because of the effort they put in to get the crystals. So then Kevin, Luke, Rhys and Steve started to live in that house and decorate it with crystals.

Helen Yemane
Christchurch Bentinck Primary School

THE LOST TRAINER

The school bell rang and I was glad!

I rushed towards the door through the sea of rushing children to meet Hayley, my best friend. 'I'll race you when we get outside,' Hayley screamed above the cacophony. 'We have a mountain of homework, finding out about all the past and present famous athletes, and I am going to be one of the future!'
Hmm! She would never be able to beat me, the fastest child in the whole school. After winning the town's sprinting race for the fourth year running, I was a natural.

'Guess what this year's prize is?' she teased.
'I don't know,' I replied, 'what is it?'
'Training with Paula Radcliffe,' she said with her face gleaming.
I had to win. I must win. Whatever it takes . . . I *will* win.
'It's only three days away now,' I said
'I know this is going to feel like the longest weekend of my life,' Hayley commented. 'I'm going to . . .'
Just then, something caught Hayley's eye.
'What? What is it?' I asked, very puzzled.
There was no answer, just the glazed look on her face. Eventually she spoke. 'Look at those.'
I looked over to a spot next to a litter bin. There on the ground was a pair of the most dirty, filthiest trainers ever. But there was something unusually familiar about them. 'They're Paula Radcliffe's trainers, when she was a young girl,' said Hayley.
'Well, what are you waiting for? Try them on,' I told her, 'and I'll race you!'
Hayley had them on in no time.
'On your marks. Get set. Go!' I shouted and Hayley sprinted like a cheetah and finished before I even started. I had to get them off her. I had to think quickly. I asked her if she would like to me to put them in her locker back at school, to save her from getting into trouble with her mum. I was relieved when she said, 'Oh yes please, that would be a great help. Thank you.'

I crept back into school cautiously, through the boys' toilets' window, up the stairs with my back close to the wall. I was willing to take any risk. I had to win this race. My mind was racing with ideas . . . then I had it. I crept into the science laboratory and found the container of acid. I carefully picked up the bottle and went back to the boys' toilets. I placed the trainers in one of the toilets and totally emptied the bottle over them. Slowly before my eyes, I watched as the trainers disappeared as they were eaten by the acid. I flushed the toilet and smiled. Suddenly I realised how guilty I felt. My body was numb and my legs were trembling. What have I done?

Monday morning at the racetrack there was no sign of Hayley. The starter gun fired and I had to get on with the race. Concentrating was hard as all I could think about was Hayley, but soon I fell into a pattern and I was zooming ahead of all the others. I won! But no - I cheated.

The car journey to meet Paula Radcliffe was difficult. I felt sick. I couldn't wait to meet her. She taught me techniques to improve my running.

'What is that?' she asks. 'That looks a bit like my trainer material when I was your age.'

Zakariya Modan (11)
Edinburgh Primary School

A GIRL WHO GOT OVER HER NERVES!

Friday, 20th April 2002

Dear Dad,

Today was raining and windy. School was fine. I had a bit of a fall-out. Don't worry, it was just a bit of name-calling, I'm not in trouble. I'm OK. I feel excited because I've been told I'm going to the Isle of Wight. I'm revising hard, so is Nafeesa. I've got a month left and I feel a bit nervous and worried. My teacher, Lucy, said that I don't need to worry, because I'm doing fine in every subject.

Me and Aisha had another fight. I got in trouble as always. Don't worry, I won't have another fight with her. I've got to go now, because Uncle's around, so see you when I see you. Don't worry, we're fine!

Monday, 6 May 2002

Dear Dad,

I'm fine, so is the rest of the family. Your friends are asking about you, especially Uncle.

Me and Nafeesa have got a week left till our exams. I'm not worried or nervous anymore. I don't really care about the SATs. I've done lots of practice tests and the science and maths books I got are so helpful. Whenever I get homework, the answers are all in there. Oh yeah, I forgot to tell you, I got a place at Walthamstow School for Girls. Me and Natasha are partners for the Isle of Wight trip. Lucy, Cunny, Nethi, and Lydia and Mark are coming with us.

Dad, I've got to go because Mum's cooked your favourite, chips, cod and everything else.

See ya when I see ya.

Dear Dad,

Everything is cool down here. How are things up there?

I finished my exams, they were so easy. Oh, I nearly forgot to tell you I did the extension paper for science and I answered 19 questions. Anyway, enough of that. I know you want to know if I've been in trouble or not. Well, I was in trouble at school today, I don't know why. It was Jermaine who was calling names, not me. I was also in trouble at home just because I told Aisha off. It is so unfair, she never gets in trouble. Anyway, I've got to go because Mum's cooked your favourite, chips, egg, fish and everything else, again.

Bye, see you soon, lots of love,

Saira!

Saira Khan (10)
Edinburgh Primary School

A NERVOUS TIME FOR A YEAR 6 CHILD!

Wednesday, 8th May 2002

Dear Kat,

Four days away from SATs, so worried and scared. What is going to happen? People in class are saying it's just a paper, scribble down what you know. I get really mad when they say that.

Oh yeah! Today we've been told by our Head that we're going on a trip to the Isle of Wight. Yippee . . . I am so glad all, my mind is out of SATs and onto the Isle of Wight. That's just what I needed.

Thursday, 9th May 2002

Dear Kat,

Today was a terrible day. Our deputy head had entered our class, which made my heart tinkle and my tummy swirl. He was testing us on questions of science. I was surprised at what he said. He told us that it's gonna be a big day, it made me shiver. My own teacher, who is very nice, had said not to worry. At least I'm not scared of my teacher . . . then our deputy . . . phew!

Monday, 13th May 2002

Dear Kat,

Today is the big day. Weekend's gone so quickly, then I thought, oh God . . . SATs. It was terrible. I was sitting there like an ice cube, sitting in the middle of nowhere. First I was like liquid flying everywhere, playing, and now I'm solid as a rock. What am I saying?

Atia Raja (11)
Edinburgh Primary School

THE UNCLE I'LL NEVER FORGET

Friday, 10th, 1946

Dear Kitty,

Over 1,000 people have died because of this war. I wish it would stop, nobody wants to die, why can't we just all live together? These adults are acting like kids. *Why can't you stop fighting!* It makes me feel so sick inside, I just want to hide under my duvet.

Monday, 12th, 1946

Dear Kitty,

The smoke is choking me. Today I saw it . . . as the silky, crimson, red river gushed from his head, I knew it was over! He was my favourite uncle and now he's gone because of this stupid war. Why did he have to die? I am so upset, he was the only one who understood me when I was feeling down.

Wednesday, 14th, 1946

Dear Kitty,

Mulberry Cottage. I wish we still lived there. I miss the sweet smell of the pansies and the roses, and you can't forget the mulberries.

Wednesday, 16th, 1946

Dear Kitty,

It could have been us. I suppose you have no idea of what I am talking about. You know the house next door? It got bombed, so we have to move out. We have no idea where we are going to go. My mum keeps shaking. Whenever I try to get close, she just pushes me away. Sometimes I feel as if it is my fault she has been so shaken up these past few weeks. Anyway, see ya!

Hannah-Leah Daley (11)
Edinburgh Primary School

CONFUSING TIMES

Friday, 18th May 1991

Dear Katy,

Today is my birthday, but also the last day of school. My grandma and grandad came over, they bought me a present each.

Outside is upsetting me, the killing of poor, innocent people because of this war. Buildings crushed down by fire, guns and shooting. It's like being in Hell, but worse. People dying, like today when I had a pound I peered outside. I saw a lady killed by a gunshot by a fresh army running over her, without caring. The area is a mass of dead bodies lying on the floor, or even burned bodies being destroyed.

Sunday, 25th March 1992

Dear Katy,

The war is still on and the days are getting shorter. Today is going to be the last day I'm going to see my mum and dad. I'm also going to miss my area and my friends. For the very first time I'm moving away from my family. All the children in London are going to be evacuated from the area to meet new families with other children. I was crying my eyes out when I heard the news. All I could take was a small suitcase with a couple of things. I was really going to miss my mum and dad.

Thursday, 30th January 1993

Dear Katy,

Today is the day I'm moving out of my house, or should I say my old house?

I leapt out of my house and strode down to the train station. I can't move, not even a bit. It was like being in my own world, jumping but then falling down. I was confused, very confused. I know I had to move on with life. I know that time was passing, so should I. I said goodbye to my mum and dad for the last time, then I sped into the train.

I waved goodbye to my family. I put my suitcase away in the train for the rest of the journey. I sped back to the door of the train. The train moved a little bit forward, and again and again, then it started to ride away. My mum and dad ran after the train, waving and crying.

Natasha Akram (11)
Edinburgh Primary School

A DAY IN THE LIFE OF ROBERT PIRES

Robert Pires gets up and goes to his training ground and kicks the ball around. When he is warmed up, he goes to his room to have breakfast which his wife has made for him. After he has finished his breakfast, he goes for some exercise for about half and hour, and gets ready for the match.

Pires gets fit for the match and when he is warmed up, he goes and puts his kit in his bag. He goes and takes his fork, knife and spoon and eats his lunch. After, he warms up again.

Then he waits for the coach, and when he reaches Highbury, he goes inside the ground and warms up again, on the pitch this time. Then he puts his kit on and goes in the centre.

In the first minute, Pires scores a goal for Arsenal and he is really happy, but in the 38th minute he gets injured and the team are sad. But the news reports say he will be back very soon.

Mahomed Rawat (9)
Edinburgh Primary School

A DAY IN THE LIFE OF DAVID, OUR TEACHER

I woke up at 7:00 and saw my mum was sleeping, so I went and looked at the time. I was late, so I had my hot bath and brushed my teeth clean and put on my clothes as quickly as I could.

I didn't make any noise because I didn't want to wake my mum, because she would do my hair again and give me a kiss on the cheek! I closed the door and took my car and left for work. I left a not for my mum saying I won't be late and don't cook me dinner, just have a lie down and relax. Have a nice day.

I went to school and parked my car in the middle of the playground, how silly! I went in and saw the children were doing their work really silently and I knew if they were being silent, the headteacher would be there soon.

I looked up and sat down in one of the children's chairs and asked them what they were doing.
'Maths,' they said.

Tatiana N'Dombasi (9)
Edinburgh Primary School

WHEN I WAS NERVOUS, WHAT STRUCK ME

13th May 2002

Hello mate, how are you doing? Are you worried about SATs? Yeh, I'm scared, I don't like SATs. I cannot believe that it is today. Today is the day of SATs. My maths sheet was terrible, but my second paper was fantastic. I am trying not to worry about SATs because that will make me nervous.
There are some good things that me and my mum are going to Tescos to buy for my packed lunch.

11th June 2002

I can't wait! I have to be at school in the morning at 7:30 to go to the Isle of Wight. My packing was terrible because I could not find my rucksack.

12th June 2002-07-27

I had to wake up at six o'clock because I had to get ready.

I knew I would pass my SATs!

Hamza Kayani (11)
Edinburgh Primary School

PAIN WITHIN

Sunday, 29th, 02

Dear Diary,

Today was the worst day of my life.

We went to North Circular forest and brought Yazmin with us. We had fun by racing, eating ice cream and the usual exciting stuff, then we went searching for a huge steep hill we love to ride on. We looked and looked until we finally found it.

We all agreed with me going first, Yaz going second and Dad going last. I climbed the hill and got ready. I let go of the brake and soared through the air with tremendous speed, screaming with enjoyment, then swerved to a halt and waited for Yazmin. I waited for a few seconds and heard a loud scream. I thought she must like it a lot as well. Slowly, minutes crawled past and still Yaz didn't come and I knew she should be here by now, so I decided to see what was happening. I saw my sister's bike on the floor, with the wheels still spinning. My heartbeat raced faster, like a Formula 1 driver pushing harder on the car pedal.

Where was she, what had happened to her . . ?
(I'll tell you tomorrow.)

Dean Grioli (11)
Edinburgh Primary School

MY DIARY

20th August 2001

Dear George,

I have just come back from America. Before I left for America, my mum told me that she and I are going to Saudi Arabia to live. We're going to be going to some posh British International School. She is a reception teacher. She said, 'You don't have to go. If you don't like it, come back in the Christmas holiday.' What's going to happen next?

31st August 2001

Dear George,

I am writing from the plane. My brother and his friend drove me to Heathrow, I then said my goodbyes to my sisters and brother.

1st September 2001

Dear George,

I have reached Saudi. As soon as I stepped out of the plane, a hot wind blew past my face. It felt like I was melting.

3rd September 2001

Dear George,

Today was my first day at school, it was fantastic. The school was in three sections. Lower, middle and upper. It's just so amazing, but unfortunately I have already started missing my family.

19th October 2001

Dear George,

Today was the worst day, the day that I regret for the whole week. Sunday, music and swimming. Music, everyone knows how to play recorder in my class, except me. And as for swimming, there are six Year 6 classes. Every human child knows how to swim, except for me!

4th December 2001

Dear George,

I cannot wait till December 12th. I'm going to England. My best friend Moe is going too. I just can't wait.

13th December 2001

Dear George,

Once again, I'm on the plane. I'm watching 'Shrek.' We are going to be landing shortly. How exciting!

Tauheed Ahmed (11)
Edinburgh Primary School

My Diary

24.12.98

Dear Sandra,

Hi Sandra, how have you been since I've been gone? You will never guess what my friend said to me. She said I look beautiful in my school uniform! I think I look ugly really. Anyway, we are just preparing for Christmas. My mum and I are going to get a Christmas tree.

I don't think it's going to be a brilliant day tomorrow because of all these people that misunderstood each other. Now they are fighting. It's not fair, is it Sandra? I have to go now Sandra, I will see you later. Hang on a minute, the smoke alarm. The smoke alarm is on! Oh Sandra, I'm really scared, the soldiers are hear. My mum is calling me downstairs. Don't worry, we'll be cool.

26.12.98

I told you, didn't I Sandra, this Christmas is a waste, it's horrible. Now we are in some country, we work so hard for the soldiers. Really Sandra, it's a disgrace, but the best bit is I meet my friends again. I'm feeling betrayed right now. I miss my home. My mum always says complaining doesn't get you anywhere. I didn't believe her, now I'm starting to believe it.

01.02.99

I'm sorry I haven't been around, it's so hard. You don't even get time to chat with friends. I can hear my mum crying, I think she is getting beaten. My dad always wanted to be the protector of his family and he can't bear watching his wife getting beaten. I think he's going to stop the man from beating Mum. Oh no, I'd better go and stop him. I will see you in five minutes, promise.

01.03.99

I'm sorry Sandra, I know I promised, but things have been really muddled these days. I feel like there is a part of me that is missing. My parents, they died yesterday. It's not fair, all my friends are gone, I have only got you now. Tomorrow morning, we are going back to my home town. I just want to be with my family.

25.12.03

Here we are, I've still got you, Sandra. Thank you for being a good friend. We went back to my home time, the war was over and we had a proper funeral for Mum and Dad. I'm now married with two children and guess what? All my friends are here with me. *Merry Christmas!*

In remembrance of Mum and Dad, I will never forget you, Sandra.

Melody Masara (10)
Edinburgh Primary School

UNTITLED

Saturday, 9th February 2002

Dear Hedgehog,

Today, me and my brother's girlfriend, Becky, went to the park. She started talking like Eminem and singing like Britney Spears. It was so funny! It's my birthday, and even though my brother Bryan didn't want to, Becky made him treat me to lunch. This might have been my best birthday ever!

Monday, 18th February 2002

Dear Hedgehog,

It is 10:00 at night and I have school tomorrow. First of all Becky, me, my sister Kathryn and my two brothers, Bryan and William, went out in the garden and played football. Then I went inside and Becky and I just talked and talked about my brother and herself!

Tuesday, 17th May 2002

Dear Hedgehog,

I can no longer talk about how much fun I have with Becky! I don't know how she died and I don't even want to know!

It was so sudden and now I'm not even sure who it was and I'm not sure if I should be living, if it was because of me. I can't just sit here and think of her. I have to see her, but how? Did it happen because someone drove her to this? I just hope I never find out and hope she died living a happy life. I know my brother is going to be broken-hearted. I just hope he'll live through this.

Hayley Russ (11)
Edinburgh Primary School

THE NERVOUS YEAR 6

Tuesday, 23rd June 2001

Dear Zako,

Today is my sister's birthday. I am worried a lot about my SATs, that's why I have to revise a lot. No television for a week, no playing or outings for a week. I am so worried. Just a few days ago was my brother's SATs test. He was worried a lot as well. I don't know what he got, but I am sure that he's going to get a high level.

No more chatting about that. Now let's talk about the SATs. When are you having yours?

Monday, 30th June 2001

Dear Zako,

The SATs are coming up, it's just one more day to go. I am so worried, the worst subject of all is English. I have to revise a lot about English, or I might get a 3!

Tuesday, 1st July 2001

Dear Zako,

Today is the day we're having our SATs. I am so worried, but I know I've got my lucky coin with me, so I know I might get a level four, or a five. *Ding, ding, dang, dang!* That was the worst bell I ever heard, so I ran upstairs and jumped onto my chair and got on with my SATs. It was maths, I wasn't worried at all, 'cause maths is my favourite subject. What is your favourite subject?

Handwriting, that was my second worst subject. I hate it. Looking at it, my handwriting is the worst, so I just have to try my best.

Samuel Hoque (10)
Edinburgh Primary School

BEHIND THE TRAPDOOR!

Today I went past my old place. I remember the first day we moved into it - phew! This is a story you're never going to believe.

You see, that place had a library. I had to do a bit of research for this science thing at school, so I walked into the library. It was all creepy and cold. There were cobwebs everywhere and that stupid library didn't help me, not even one little bit. All the books were about potions and all that freaky stuff.

These books got me suspicious, I didn't know why. *Thump!* There was a sudden noise that made me jump to my feet. I really like to investigate, like the people on TV, so I crept up the crooked staircase. The noise sounded as if it was in my new room, and it was!

I peeped into the little holes in my door. There, I saw a white frost of mist. I ran down the stairs as fast as I could, I wanted someone to help me, so I called my friend Tracy over.

When she arrived, we both stumbled up the crooked staircase and opened my bedroom door. There beneath our feet was a thing. It looked like a trapdoor! We struggled to open it. It didn't even budge. When we finally opened it, there was this long, long, long staircase with little specks of light on the sides. There were also portraits of these old Tudor people. It took me and Tracy a long time to get to the bottom.

When we did get to the bottom, there was this awful smell and the frost of mist was there as well. We looked at each other, confused, and marched down the long passageway. Then there was this noise, this noise that made me feel cold. The white mist was getting stronger and stronger and then the noise again. I hated it. Tracy hated it.

Suddenly, a shadow was approaching us, a white shadow. Me and Tracy shouted and screamed. We both ran up the long, long, long staircase and shut the trapdoor, but the white shadows were rising. I then realised they must be the *spirits of the Tudor dead!*

I grabbed Tracy by the hand and we both tumbled down the stairs. We were both in shock. The spirits were following us down the stairs, there was no way to get out!

We ran to the library and shut the door, but it didn't help. The spirits were coming and coming. The books! I then remembered they were about magic. We didn't have any time to look. Tracy and me tore open the books, looking for chants or spells. We couldn't find anything. But then I found the most lovely book I had ever seen. It was beautiful, with gold and diamonds, but I had no time to admire it, the spirits were approaching us.

I ripped open the book and read out chants and poems. It was then I realised the spirits were sinking to the ground. Me and Tracy jumped with all our might and ran upstairs. In my bedroom, the trapdoor disappeared before our very own eyes. We were safe, but not forever.

Farha Sonvadi (10)
Edinburgh Primary School

MARY, MARY

Jack's dead! Fool! I can't believe we have to stand in the rain because of some idiot that got himself killed. Actually, I quite fancied him . . . when he was alive! And I had to lend the church my silver bells and my maids. I can't believe they think eight maids can carry a man with their high heels on. And I need to go to work so I can buy that Kitty Kat club. I'm going home. Oh yeah, what car have I got? Yes, my Land Rover.

The funeral's finished and I'm driving home, but something's wrong. I keep on having funny visions of my dead flat-renter, Jack. Phew, I'm home. I'd better be careful in case I fall into a trance, then I walk out of my flat and onto the top of my roof garden and . . . but that will never happen. I'm finally home, but there's a hole in my door. I open my door, then I see it. My house is trashed.

I tidied it up. I also found a bit of paper, I threw it away. But that was the thing I regretted most. Then I got a phone call. It was him. I was spooked. It was about the piece of paper. When he cut off, I rummaged through the bin for the vital piece of paper. I found it. I was doomed.

Jourdane DeCourcy-Nolan (11)
Edinburgh Primary School

WHY?

Wednesday, 19th, 1945

Dear Secret,

Today is the end of my life. It is the end of the world. What's the worth of wars? I hate them, everyone hates them!

I'm being evacuated today. My bag and box (the little wooden one) are waiting for me to take them to a stranger's home, but if I pray enough, I just might go somewhere better than this house. If I pray enough I might, just might, get someone better than Mum.

I'm leaving now. I know I'm not going to get any goodbyes. I would get one if Dad was here, but he's not. He's dead.

Monday, 24th, 1945

Dear Secret,

I'm in Mr Bill Herring's house. The house in itself is tiny. My bedroom consists of a small straw bed, a wooden cupboard, a table with an oil lamp on it and nothing else, not even a rag rug, but I must always be thankful. No matter what, at least Mr Bill looks after me properly. At least he's better than Mum.

Thursday, 11th, 1947

Dear Secret,

I'm at home all alone. Not one soul beside me - why? Why doesn't anybody love me? They have all gone to the party down the road, I'm on my own, all alone. Oh no, she's here. I'd better go!

Irfana Patel (11)
Edinburgh Primary School

First Time To Leave My Mum

Thursday, 5th June

Dear Diary,

Only three days to go! I can't wait to go to the Isle of Wight on the eighth! It will be so exciting, we are going to do some fun activities. It will be a beautiful, exciting day to sleep in a 'dorm' as they say in the fantastic brochure. It will be just like Harry Potter!

I've been spending my time packing my bags. I'm worried about the journey because it might take seven or ten hours. I might feel sick. My mum's worried, scared, unhappy and sad because she's going to miss me so much. I am gonna miss my whole family for three days.

Monday, 9th June

At last I've got to the Isle of Wight. First to start with the fun activities. I can do anything - swim in the floaty pool, sleep in the cosy bunk bed and climb a fantastic tree.

What a great place!

Mehtab Yousaf (10)
Edinburgh Primary School

A DAY I'LL NEVER FORGET!

I was so nervous! My heart was pounding and my feet felt like jelly. I swallowed hard. I knew that soon the moment would come. I had placed myself on a chair in the waiting room. I was frightened at the thought of having my tonsils removed. Time was ticking past . . . Minutes felt like seconds and the silence made me shiver. I took a tight hold of my mum's hand.

I closed my eyes. I was trying not to remind myself about the operation, but it wouldn't help. The word 'operation' kept coming back. I began to lose control of myself, I was acting like a terrified toddler. Clip, clop, clip, clop, I heard the sound of rubber soles squeaking on the varnished floor. That's what made me open my eyes. It was a nurse, she had a clipboard in her hand and she read, 'Jessica Daley? The doctor would like to see you now.'

She led me towards the doctor's room, where a bed stood in the corner with white, crisp sheets pulled over its pointed corners. It was beckoning me towards it. My mind wandered off to dreamland. Suddenly, I heard the doctor's voice. He was telling me to lie down on the bed. I walked unsteadily towards it and lay on it, feeling extremely nervous.

After a few hours I woke up, relieved to know that the operation was over. That's when I realised that the pain inside my throat was making my eyes water.

My life in hospital was identical to Hell. The food they fed me was like cold cabbage. The bed they made me sleep in was so hard, it made me feel like I was sleeping on a flat rock. I was overjoyed when I heard I could go home, when I heard I could eat normal food, when I heard I could sleep in a normal bed and when I heard I could live a normal life.

Muneeba Munawar (11)
Edinburgh Primary School

A Day In The Life Of A Pineapple

One day I was sitting relaxed. I was very happy, I thought I would have another lazy day. My eyes were closing, when a nasty man came running up to me, then I got pulled out of the ground. Ouch! That hurts, I thought.

Then those nasty men threw me into a huge thing and they closed the door. I was thinking they would kill me. I fell off a basket. The dark place was moving, I started bumping into things. I got hurt badly by a piece of metal. That nasty man tried to hold me and squeeze me so hard, so I cut him with my spiky, sharp leaves.

I thought the man was a witch. The witch shouted, 'Three pounds a pineapple.' I thought the man was crazy.
'How much money for one pineapple?' said a man.
The witch said, 'Three pounds.'
At last I'm free from those witches. Then I was astonished, I heard the children saying, 'When will we eat the pineapple?' Then it was night, I couldn't sleep. Then they cut my skin off, sliced me up, I said goodbye, that was the end.

Hadika Maqsood (9)
Edinburgh Primary School

A DAY IN THE LIFE OF A RABBIT

I woke up one morning and had a huge stretch. I came out from my small, cosy, quiet warren. I thought this would be a normal day, but suddenly there was a big, loud *bang!* I quickly ran inside my warren.

I hopped over to a little stream and had a huge sip of water. Then I went over to a mini waterfall and washed under it. Next, I went out for exercise by hopping over to another warren where my other rabbit friend lived. I woke her up and she felt very happy to see me.

Me and my friend went over to a field, we grabbed a few vegetables and hopped off. We had eaten some of the food and stored the rest in our warrens.

Then we saw a hunter, as big as a giant! We got really scared. We were having lunch in our warrens when some bears came and chased the giant. We went out and saw the giant leaving. We were happy.

We ate our dinner and then we snuggled up in our warrens and slept.

Nayyar Ali (9)
Edinburgh Primary School

A DAY IN THE LIFE OF THE ROCK

One boiling day, I woke up at 12am and I couldn't even move a muscle. I told my butler to help me up, then I thought of an idea.

I quickly brushed my teeth and jumped in my very own swimming pool. This got the blood pumping around my body. At 1pm I went to an expensive restaurant in a limousine. 'Can I please have your autograph?' Loud voices came all around my limousine.
'Drive!' I bellowed.
' But . . . but . . .'
'No buts, you fool!' I yelled even louder.
'But Sir, there are people in front as well.'
'Use the horn and if they don't move, *run over them!*' I screeched in my loudest voice. It was just my luck, they moved when they heard the horn. After a big, delicious lunch of lobster and a big fish, I forgot all about the loud autograph hounds.

I went to the gym where my wrestling friends were. In the gym, I did some exercise and practised my special moves. It was finally 8pm, so I went to WWE where a special event was being held. It was called 'Judgement Day', where I fought in a re-match against Hollywood Hulk Hogan. I still beat him and went home feeling very proud. When I got there, I went to sleep with a smile on my face.

Tanish Chaudry (9)
Edinburgh Primary School

A DAY IN THE LIFE OF JENNIFER LOPEZ

The sun was shining, she got up and demanded, 'Servant, get me dressed in my swimming kit.'
'OK.'
She got dressed, washed her face, had breakfast and brushed her teeth. She had a lovely jacuzzi and she was relaxing, then she got dressed and went to the place where she practised her songs. And then her servant drove to the mall.

After she went shopping and bought a new dress and jewellery, she went home and then she got dressed in her new dress and went to her husband and said, 'Quickly, get ready, I don't' want to be late.'
So he got dressed and they went to a famous restaurant.

In the restaurant, there were many famous people and then people had to sing. Jennifer Lopez was the first, she sang 'Ain't It Funny,' and everybody liked her song. She was so tired, she went to sleep.

Next day there was a knock on the door. She opened the door and her new single was out and had reached number one! She was so excited and celebrated all night long.

Anisa Fazal (8)
Edinburgh Primary School

A DAY IN THE LIFE OF CLAIRE FROM STEPS

As I woke up at 7am, I went straight to my jacuzzi. When I got out, I had to feed my cat, Sassy. Next, my butler drove me to the studio.

When I got out, lots of people came up to me asking for my autograph, so I had to give my autograph before I went inside. When I finally got inside, I felt very tired and weak in my right hand. Anyway, I performed my song 'DJ' with H.

After, my video was recorded. I had to do it another three times before it was on TV.

After, I went shopping with my butler, called Tolola, and H. I told Tolola to get me some sprays, perfume and clothes (fashionable, nice clothes.) When I got out, H drove me home.

I asked if H would like to stay round my house. H said he'd love to. For dinner, we went to a famous restaurant. Me and H went to bed at 11pm, we were shattered.

Kelly Drury (9)
Edinburgh Primary School

A DAY IN THE LIFE OF A WATERMELON

One day, I was sleeping on the ground, when I woke up to a nice, frosty, fresh morning. After five or ten minutes of a nice lie in, the farmer came and sprinkled water, to feed me my breakfast.

At about eight o'clock, the farmer came along and pulled me out of the ground very harshly. He then started squeezing me and shaking me to check if I had enough juice in me. With this, I was getting very angry and disturbed.

I was then thrown into a big, hard cardboard box and dumped into a huge van. After, I had a very bumpy ride to the high street. I was very displeased.

After a long wait in the van, I was finally taken and thrown into a big pile of watermelons. Lots of people came and picked me up, but nobody bought me. I wished I was in my farm.

The store was just about to close, when someone said, 'Please Sir, can I buy this watermelon?' I was then bought and carried home.

After a little while I was all cut up. My juice and everything was squeezed out and I got eaten. Munch, munch, munch.

That was the end of my day.

Zuleikha Anwar (9)
Edinburgh Primary School

A Day In The Life Of A Cheetah

One lazy day at about 4am I woke up with a big stretch. I went to hunt the deer, so I camouflaged myself in the grass. They heard me, so they ran and then I ran with all my power and caught two big ones and two small ones.

I gave the small ones to the cubs, and the two big ones, the big cheetahs ate. Then I went to a lake and had a little scoop of it and went up a tree and fell asleep, because of all that running. Zzzzz . . .

When I woke up I went home, but my family wanted me to hunt again because they were hungry. I didn't agree, so we started to fight. We were scratching each other.

Then me and my brother went to hunt for antelopes, so we went to camouflage ourselves in the grass. We ran and caught one each and brought them home and we all ate. After, we all went to bed and had nice dreams!

Yazmin Grioli (9)
Edinburgh Primary School

A DAY IN THE LIFE OF A CARROT

One lay day, I woke up at 4am. I was very bored, so I went to sit in the field. Suddenly, the farmer came along, picked me up and squashed me to see if I was alright to eat. He then took me to the market and put me on sale.

Some people came along, picked me up and squashed me to check if I was alright to eat. I thought they were very nice people, they thought I was alright, so they gave the farmer the money, put me in a plastic bag and carried me home.

As soon as we got home, they put me in a basket. I was very frightened and scared. I did not know what they were going to do with me. After ten minutes, they got some salad, cucumber, lettuce, tomato. They cut me in two pieces. I was put on a plate, I didn't have any idea of what they were going to do with me.

Suddenly, they picked me up and picked a knife. They cut my skin first, then my head, put it on a plate, picked up my skin and gave it to the rabbit for dinner. They both ate me for carrot supper. Unfortunately my day ended with me being eaten - crunch, crunch.

The next day they went to the farmer to get my brothers and sisters.

Mayra Azam (9)
Edinburgh Primary School

WHY SATS?

8th May 2002

Dear Diary,

I am four days away from my SATs! Everyone's talking about it, I'm not bothered yet. My friends are all worried about it. Here's my tip, just revise at home as much as you can and when it's done, it's done.

15th May 2002

Last night, I was trying to learn my times tables. I was sitting at a table and in front of me was a pink piece of paper. My hand was struggling and I didn't know what to write.

10th May 2002

Thank God it's over, I don't want to do that again. After break, we're doing a spelling test. I hope I just do well.

Nida Syed (10)
Edinburgh Primary School

BELLE'S BEAST

The day before yesterday, a girl called Belle and her father vanished. No one knows what happened to them. Some people say that they might have run away.

Belle's sisters Agnieszka and Jennifer say that Belle went out yesterday to look for their dad. They knew she loved her father so much she went to find him.

The villagers accused the beast that lives up on the mountain. Yesterday, Belle's father came running from the mountain shouting, 'The beast has captured my daughter.'

The angry villagers got huge logs and marched to the rescue. Finally, the villagers got to the beast's castle. They sat on the logs. Belle was inside having fun.

Whilst the others were sleeping, Belle's father sneaked inside the castle. He told Belle what was going to happen. Belle was terrified. 'They can't do that!' cried Belle.
Her father said, 'You'd better warn the beast.'
Just then, the villagers woke up, picked up the logs and used them to ram into the door, just like when two rams butt each other.

Then the villagers broke in and ransacked the place. The beast fought to keep them out, but one villager, Dan King, ran up to the tower and attacked the beast. Belle tried to stop them fighting but Dan pushed Belle and Belle fell. Belle shouted to the beast and the beast caught Belle's hand and pulled her up. Dan jumped on him. The beast threw Dan off the cliff, then the beast fell to his knees and turned into a handsome teenager. Then Belle and the beast kissed, got married and lived happily ever after.

Shameelah Siddeeq (11)
Edinburgh Primary School

GHOST OF WINTER

He came out on winter's nights, nobody knew what it was because it always had a mask on. When night came, he came out and broke into people's houses and stole their money. If there was no money he would trash the place, then move on to the next house. There was a man watching tele and he heard the door slam and he got up and hid. The Ghost of Winter was looking for money and he found it and ran away. The next night he came back to the same house and the man tried to catch the Ghost of Winter with a net, but with no luck. Then the ghost ran away. He came to the same house the next day and the man set some traps. He made a boxing glove and put it by the door and, when the ghost came, he ran straight into the boxing glove because it was on a string. The man phoned the police and he was sent to prison. The people were glad because they weren't poor anymore.

Jordan Gibling (10)
Falconbrook Primary School

LEE AND POTT - THE TWO SPACE BOYS

Lee and Pott are on holiday and want to have a great time. Pott and Lee want to explore. First they go to a shopping centre. They have a look at a pizza. Someone comes around the corner and screams. Her mouth is open. She faints. Pott takes her money and goes and buys the pizza. Pott and Lee eat the pizza hungrily.

They go to the park and go inside a shed. Inside the shed there are lots of golf clubs and bags covered with moss. The bags are like a big bunch of flowers. After investigating the shed, Pott and Lee go to the pond.

Pott drops his tissue and a duck picks it up. The duck waddles away with Pott thundering after him. In the water goes the duck.
Lee shouts, 'Stop!' but all too late, Pott is already in the water and is sinking fast.
Lee looks all around him and sees a large log. He throws it in the water and shouts, 'Grab on.'
Pott holds on tight while Lee pulls with all his might. Suddenly Pott's head can be seen. Then Pott's body emerges. Out comes Pott.
'Oh Pott, you're OK,' says Lee.
Pott says, 'I think we've had a good holiday, don't you?'
'Yes,' agrees Lee and they walk off back to their ship.

James Fell & Mohammed Hussein (9)
Flora Gardens School

Trapped On Earth

After doing a nosedive through the fifth solar system, I landed on a peculiar planet called *School!* We walked around and then we saw a strange transparent material. I went up to it and looked through it. Inside we saw outlandish black and white creatures.

As I turned around I saw a big, hard stick, with baby sticks coming out of it. When I looked up I saw grey and white blobs drifting in the sky. When I put my head down to normal, I saw two cuboids stuck together with a tent stuck on top.

Also when I looked a bit to the right, I saw hundreds of little green life forms on more baby sticks. I was in this weird area with clusters of sticks. As soon as I was getting out of this area, hundreds of little green creatures just like the ones we saw through the material all came running towards me as I was running towards the exit.

I got out just in time. But outside this strange area was worse than inside it. Hundreds more creatures were walking around. One of the creatures walked past me and screamed and fainted. We walked a little further and we saw a building called Bank. We went inside this building called Bank.

Everyone made a screeching noise and ran away. There were no more creatures except for one. It was blue and had a shiny mark on its chest. It was coming towards me, it held me in its tentacle and walked over to the exit. It *kicked* me right out of the building onto a grey circular tube.

I got out and saw another big building. I went inside and saw lots of human food. I went a bit further and saw lots of humans' tools. I took a few of them and got out of this weird place, but the problem was we didn't know where our ship was. I tried to ask one of the creatures, but as soon as we said a word, it ran away. So we walked until our feet died down which was where our ship was.

We walked over to it, we got out the tools, then we started to fix the ship. We happened to fix the ship quite quickly thanks to the humans' tools. So we used our ship to get back home and live happily ever after.

Sarwar Ali (8) & Amir-Ali Bazazi (9)
Flora Gardens School

THE SECRET OF THE GOONIES

It all happened one afternoon. Two children called Zap and Zoë stayed in the playground. They heard a mean, hideous laugh. They went in the school, they went nearer and nearer to the hall.

At last they got to the hall. They put one foot in the hall and saw . . . the teachers but not the same - they were monsters. They had green eyes and one long line of blue hair.

The teacher chased Zap. Zoë ran back to the gate. Mum and Dad were there. Zoë catching her breath said to Dad, 'Zap is being chased by monsters, think of a good idea!' *Pss pss*. Zap was just about to be eaten . . . but Zoë came in through the window because the door was locked and would not open without a key.

They escaped through the window and ran to Mum and Dad as fast as they could.

Ahmed Jumale (8) & Karl de St Aubin (9)
Flora Gardens School

MY ADVENTURE

I arrived on planet Earth in a strange enclosure. My name is Odle. I am a chatty, adventurous person and I'm ten years old. I have a sister who is four years old, called Mo. She is scared of Two-Leggers because she is not used to them and she is frightened by them. My dad is a strong man, he is brave and intelligent, but he is extremely nervous where we have landed, because there are a lot of Two-Leggers.

We stepped out of the spacecraft and looked around, we saw the Two-Leggers in front of us, so we ran into an empty house, but the Two-Leggers were catching up fast. We tried furiously to run, but then all of a sudden, a strange sensation came over Odle. The Two-Leggers had put their feet on us and wiped their feet around Mo. Mo screamed as loud as she could and the Two-Leggers ran after her. Dad ran after them. He pulled Mo out of their arms. After he got Mo, we ran through the front door because there were dogs belonging to the Two-Leggers trying to catch us as well.

We ran out of the back door of the house. After we ran out of the house, we saw our spacecraft, but we didn't want to go to our planet called Alangolia very early, because we had just arrived and the fun had just begun. We lost the Two-Leggers and thought of a plan to catch them. So we built a trap that we are going to tell you about. First we made a model of ourselves, so they would think that it is us. Then we put a net over the sculptures and when they push the sculptures, the net will fall on them, then we will have caught the Two-Leggers. After an hour they came and pushed the sculptures, the net fell on them and at last we caught them. We took them to our planet and the reason we took them is because we wanted them to be our slaves, and if they didn't do as we told them, we would gobble them up!

Nataleigh Taylor (9) & Romina Fatemi (8)
Flora Gardens School

THE LOST KEY

In came Harry and Melanie from school, exhausted from the days of work. Harry wanted to complete his portrait and Melanie to give more ideas, but he couldn't do anything to make Melanie accept. Melanie wasn't a child like him, not at all. She was his best friend, but didn't help because her personality was totally different. She was tall, playful and she didn't take things seriously, I mean it! Nothing like Harry! Look at Harry; he was intelligent, anxious and most of all, adventurous. He always wanted to be a detective, well something like that! It was his childhood dream! He couldn't carry on with Melanie. She was flopping about in this moment and wanted to play in the funfair that was just on.

Melanie forced Harry to go with her. But Harry wouldn't let her go with it now! He made her trip over, Melanie pushed him over on the ground,.Harry started to enjoy this and a sparkling mirror in the corner of his bedroom caught his eye, he had a very thoughtful idea of a nasty attack . . . Harry didn't know what he was doing and the next minute, he knocked Melanie (who was just getting up from her rest) into the hard and stiff mirror. Harry thought that Melanie would have a terrible bruise and no Miss Annoying! But instead of Melanie tumbling down to the floor, she just went through the mirror, just went through it!

Harry got out of his mean and horrible mood and thought what he should do next to help Melanie. The first thing he thought he would do was to go up to the mirror and go through it as well, but Harry didn't have enough guts to finish off his life in just a second. He stared at it, thinking what Melanie was doing. Then a big storm came out of the dusty mirror and swept Harry into the imaginary world.

Harry and Melanie opened their eyes and found that they were in a cottage. Shocked and amazed, they looked at each other when in came a farmer. They were told that they were found on the beach and this kind farmer brought them into his small cottage. The first thing he said was, 'Hello young ones, did you read the newspaper? Ooh yes, of course you didn't' the farmer stopped talking for a few seconds and started again. 'It said that two children arrived at this beach and to go back to their home, they have to find a key. It's quite stupid, but there it is!' Harry and Melanie were amazed at first, but they reckoned that those two children were them! They had to find the key anyway to go back, they didn't want to miss their holiday.

The next moment they went to search for the key on the beach. Harry looked around the edge of the sea and Melanie searched over a hill on the beach. They looked and looked until it was midnight. They gave up searching for the night and slept peacefully, they dreamt of lots of things they could've done in the holidays. The next morning, they were starving and the farmer offered some fish. Harry loved fish but didn't know where the farmer would get them. Suddenly the farmer started to laugh and cried out, 'We're going fishing!' Harry and Melanie started to cheer.

When they reached the place where the farmer liked to fish, there were lots of fish. They took a hole bunch and were on the way home to eat it. Harry had three and started to eat. He enjoyed the first two, but he didn't quite enjoy the third because there was something hard in it. *Something hard in it! The key!* So now they were able to go back. When Harry touched the key, he found that he and Melanie were at home. They had a wonderful holiday!

Abida Rahimi (9) & Jamie Joahill (8)
Flora Gardens School

THE MONSTER

Natalie's house backs onto railway arches with a thin alley between her garden wall and one of the arches. One day, when she had absolutely nothing to do, she decided to climb the wall of her small, dull garden.

She scrambled to the top of the wall and stopped for breath. Natalie looked up and gasped. Instead of seeing the towering black arches, she saw another world, where she met a girl called Bashira.

Whilst they were trying to find their way through thick woods, they came across a huge castle. Very frightened, they decided to enter as heavy rain started to fall. They were unaware that the castle was haunted.

In the middle of the night, a monster came and he looked hairy and sneaky. The monster was trying to get them, but he didn't. They thought and thought how to get the monster trapped.

Ding!

'I know, we could try to put a magic box over him,' said Bashira.

They discovered the magic box in a gloomy room covered with cobwebs and silver dust. When the monster was sleeping, they sneaked up behind it and threw the large, golden box over the monster's head. Magically, the monster shrank.

Bashira went out of the haunted castle and got into an aeroplane to go to another world and Natalie went into another aeroplane that went into her world, so she got home safely.

Bashira Meah & Natalie Pearson (9)
Flora Gardens School

MASUMA'S VISIT

Masuma is a brave nine year old girl. It is night-time and Masuma is asleep in her warm, comfy, cosy bed. She wakes up and goes to the kitchen to get a drink because she is really thirsty. It is cold and dark and Masuma feels very scared. She switches on the kitchen light, but nothing happens. She finds a torch in the cupboard but there are no batteries init. Masuma makes her way to the fridge in the dark. She opens the door and to her amazement, the fridge is bare. Masuma hears someone or something snoring behind her. She turns around very slowly and there asleep on the floor is a monster. The monster is very ugly and with blue, scaly skin and huge pointed teeth. There is a nasty smell coming from the beast. It is like a boys' toilet. The monster beings to stir and then it wakes up. Masuma screams and turns around to run back the to safety of her bedroom. Suddenly she feels someone pulling her backwards, she spins around thinking that the monster has got her, only to find that she is in the safety of her mum's arms. It is then that Masuma realises that she has been sleep-walking and having a terrible nightmare.

Maryam Zarif, Masuma Ahmed & Lena Samirie (9)
Flora Gardens School

THE SECRET MYSTERY BEHIND THE MIRROR

Holly was in her room. She looked in her mirror. The mirror was framed glittery silver. Holly put her hand on the mirror. Suddenly, her hand went through it. Holly felt surprised because she did that a lot of times, but her hand never went through. She put her leg in too, then she entered. It was dark, Holly thought it was a tunnel the floor was rocky and rough. She went a step further, then two or three steps more. Suddenly Holly saw two small, ragged children - they looked like urchins or chimney sweeps in the books on Victorian children she had seen at school.

Holly wondered what they were doing in this mysterious place. The two children introduced themselves.
'I'm Harry,' said one of the children, grinning.
'I'm Lucy,' said the other child.
Holly didn't like the look of them and didn't want to be in a strange place somewhere through her bedroom mirror. 'I . . . I . . . have to go back home for my dinner,' blurted Holly and turned to walk back through the mirror.
'*What* mirror?' asked the two ragged children.
'The one where I came from, my bedroom.'
'*What* bedroom?'
'Oh never mind.'

Harry, Lucy and Holly all calmed down. They went to sleep on the rocky floor which was very uncomfortable. The time passed by. It came to be the middle of the night. Lucy woke up and heard a thundering noise. She went to find out what the noise was. Lucy could not see what was making the noise because dust was going in her eyes. The noise was getting louder. Then she saw something coming closer to her. She heard a foot banging against the rocky floor. Bang, bang, bang. Suddenly it stopped. Just then, Lucy realised what it was. It was a *three-headed cat!*

It had claws like needles, also it had yellow eyes, like jewels. Lucy screamed so loud that the cat's eardrums got blocked.

Holly and Harry woke up.
'What was all that *screaming?*' yelled Holly and Harry together.
Lucy was so scared that she fainted. Holly and Harry saw the three-headed cat. 'Uh oh, spagghetioes,' gasped Holly and Harry. Harry found a knife and quickly stabbed the three-headed cat. Holly ran over to the other end of the room to see if Lucy was okay. Lucy was fine, she woke up. Holly tried to go through the mirror one more time. Her leg went through. Holly said goodbye to Harry and Lucy, then she entered here whole body back through the mirror. Holly was glad to be home again.

Aicha Jaowad, Sophie Stanley (8) & Katie Pemberton (9)
Flora Gardens School

The Great Battle

Myran went to the park on a very cold, wet, rainy day to go to his football club. A couple of hours later, his team lost 2-0, but by then the rain had died away and his mum let him play for a while. He saw a huge tree he had not seen before, so he went to inspect it.

To his surprise there was a hole big enough for him to fit into, so he went inside. When he got inside, the hole crashed shut and the inside started to shake and rumble. After that a big crack opened up and he fell down it. When he landed on the ground, he saw a big crowd of angry men dressed in combat gar with weapons like bows, swords and axes. They all shouted, 'Ready commander!'
'What?' asked Myran.
'You're our commander.'
'Am I? Okay then,' he cried in a surprised way.

'It looks like there's going to be a battle,' Myran said.
'Yes there is,' said the men.
'I don't know how to be a commander,' exclaimed Myran, 'but I'll have a go.'
Right then a big noise came from the other side of a hill. A big cloud of dust came flying at the army and then Myran's army said, 'Commence attack!'

The two armies started running at each other. Myran didn't know what to do. Then a soldier came up to him and gave him a sword and told him the basic moves. After that someone came up to him and attacked him, but luckily, one of Myran's army men came and set him free, so he could geet to the other king's castle.

Once Myran got to the castle gates, he had a feeling that someone, or something, was waiting for him, and when he got in the castle he was right . . . there was a dragon! At least he thought there was, but it was only a picture. A few hours later when he finally got to the thronen room, the king wasn't there . . .

To be continued . . .

Pida Ahmed & Myran Maughan-Dineen (8)
Flora Gardens School

The Dream

There was once a girl named Tiffany. Tiffany always had a dream that she would become famous. She had this dream over and over and over. One day, Tiffany went to her room and looked up at the sky. She wished in her head, it is my heart's desire to be famous and I know it will come true.

Tiffany went into the kitchen and started crying as she looked at her favourite singers. Suddenly things started to feel weird and Tiffany felt like she was being pulled. She felt like she was trapped and being dragged along. Then Tiffany realised, she was on the road to fame and fortune. This is how Tiffany's adventure began!

'Oh my word, where am I? Am I in Heaven? This is not my bedroom!' Tiffany exclaimed. She didn't realise that she was standing right in front of a limo, until the driver came out. When Tiffany hopped inside the limo, she felt a strange pulling feeling again. What's happening? Where am I going? Tiffany thought. She then caught a glimpse of her reflection in the tinted window. Tiffany was changing. It finally stopped and *bang!*

Tiffany found herself in a strange room. She looked at the door and it said, 'Tiffany's Dressing Room.' Tiffany went back inside and looked in the mirror. She looked taller and her face was different. Tiffany realised she was older.
Then a strange man entered the room. 'Hey, Ms Tiffany, here are your clothes. You're on in five minutes. Why don't you wear something to match your Grammy Award?'
Tiffany froze. She was trying to talk. 'G . . .g . . . Grammy Award?'
The man looked shocked. 'Why yes. You've won two for the best female singer and best dancer of the year.'
Wow! thought Tiffany, can this really be true?

It wasn't long until Tiffany's name was called out for the Grammy Awards she had won. This is what she said . . .

'Wow, thank you. This is a great honour. I never thought I would be standing here. This has been my heart's desire and I've had this dream ever since I was little, now I know that dreams really do come true!

Chituru Osumah (10)
Glenbrook Junior School

CRAZY FOOTBALL

Once upon a time there was a boy called Chris. Chris wanted to bring a football team together, but he needed help from his friend. One Saturday morning, Christopher went to his friend Daniel's house. He said, 'Do you want to be on my football team?'
'Oh, yes please!' said Daniel.
So Chris told Daniel to come to football training next Tuesday and Thursday.

Next, Christopher went to Denton's house. Christopher rang on the doorbell but the bell wasn't working. Chris knocked on the letter box and was finally let in. When Chris walked into the house, Denton was singing, 'I gotta get through this, I gotta get through this . . .' Chris asked Denton if he'd like to be on his football team. Denton was happy to join the team, but only if he could play in defence.

It was now 6:30 in the evening and Chris still had one more person to see. The last person was Luke. Luke was a very good goalkeeper. When he got to his house, he was watching a Chelsea vs Man U football match. Luke looked sad because Chelsea lost 3-0.
'Luke, do you want to be on my football team?' asked Chris.
Luke wanted to know who was going to be coach and Chris told him that his father would do it. Luke agreed to play, although he only wanted to play midfield or goalkeeper.

Chris was waiting to ask the rest of his friends to play tomorrow, as he had to get home for dinner.

The next day, Chris went to Mohammed's house. 'Mohammed, would you like to be on my football team?' asked Chris.
Mohammed also agreed, as long as he could be the striker.

Chris' dad organised the rest of the team and they were all ready for their first training session the following Tuesday. At training, Chris' dad got them to do some simple skills like dummying your opponent. To start with, the coach thought the team were all a bit crazy. He yelled out, 'Have another go!' The second time, the team did the drill very well. Christopher trained the team and his dad trained Luke, the goalkeeper. The team were very skilful.

On Thursday, the coach said there was a match on Saturday. 'Please don't play on Saturday how you played on Tuesday because you played crazy,' said Coach.
Everyone said, 'But that's our style, it's our good luck charm to play crazy.'
'Dad, who are we playing?' asked Christopher.
'Rosendale,' he replied.
Rosendale were not very good. Their strikers were very weak.
'What time do we have to meet?'
'We'll meet at 10am and we will be leaving at 10:15 sharp!' said Dad.

Saturday morning came, everyone turned up on time. They had a quick practice before the match. Soon the match began and they got off to a crazy start. The goalkeeper kicked the ball to Mohammed and he then took a crazy shot. It hit the crossbar and bounced off onto the post.
'Goal!' shouted Mohammed.
Coach said, 'That was crazy!'
It was almost half-time before they scored a goal. It was Daniel from the half-way line.

At half-time, Coach said they were playing crazy, but he said that was good because they were winning. He said to keep it up in the second half. During the second half, the team played really well. *E* had another try, but their goalkeeper managed to save it. Rosendale scored in the 84th minute. It was now very nerve-racking.

Final whistle blew! They had won! They were so happy, everyone sprayed their water everywhere.
'Well done, boys, winning that match has put you at the top of the table,' said Coach. 'Our next match is in two weeks' time, make sure you play as well and we'll soon win the league.'

Christopher Cole (10)
Glenbrook Junior School

The Mysterious Treasure?

Just outside Dan's bedroom door, there was a floorboard that squeaked as though it was protesting about being trodden on. Dan was walking along the landing on his way to his bedroom, when it squeaked again.
'Mum, that floorboard is really bugging me.'
Mum replied, 'I will try and fix it in the summer holidays, OK.'
'I wonder why it's making that noise anyway?' Dan whispered anxiously. Maybe it's a bit loose, he thought to himself.

Dan walked up to the floorboard and pressed it very gently. *Skreek!* The noise got louder and then the floorboard flipped up just an inch from Dan's mouth. There was a long hole in the floor where the floorboard had lifted. Dan put his hand in and felt something strange. He pulled the peculiar thing out of the hole. It was a round piece of wood with an ancient-looking symbol on it. That's strange, thought Dan, this is the same symbol I learnt about in school and it was on a bag of ancient money that someone had hidden before they died a long time ago.

Dan put his hand back in the hole to see if he could find something else. He found two more things: a smelly sock which he did not expect, and a bag full of gold coins. The coins were as big as three two pound coins stuck together. 'Wow!' said Dan in amazement. Dan heard his mum's footsteps coming up the stairs. In a flash, Dan put everything back in the hole, forgetting to put back the smelly sock.
'Dan, what's that disgusting, awful smell?' asked Mum.
'I don't know, maybe it's my feet?' Dan replied anxiously.
Then Mum yelled, 'Well, you'd better wash them, *now!*'

When Dan got to school, he told his friends about his discovery and as soon as they finished school, they rushed back to Dan's house.
'Dan, what are all your friends doing here?' asked Mum.
'We're doing a project together. Don't worry, and sorry I didn't tell you earlier. Bye.'
In a flash, the boys were all upstairs.
'Where is it then?' asked one of Dan's friends.
'Yeah, and what's that nasty smell? It's worse than ten people letting off wind!' said another friend.

Dan carefully lifted the floorboard. He reached inside but was unable to find anything. Where is it? Dan thought to himself.
'There's nothing here. Thanks for wasting our time!' yelled Dan's friends.
'Wait, I had it for real, I promise,' pleaded Dan.
Dan's friends left in a grumpy mood.
'Is this what they were looking for?' asked Mum, holding up the bag of coins.
'Where did you get that?' Dan exclaimed.
'I knew about it all along and I didn't tell you, as I knew you would tell everybody and I didn't want that to happen,' said Mum.
'Thanks Mum, now all my friends think I'm a liar!' replied Dan.
'I think we should keep this quiet and to ourselves so we can enjoy the fortune,' said Mum.
'OK,' answered Dan.
So Dan and his mum lived happily on their fortune of ancient gold coins. Maybe Dan would hide the remainder of the coins somewhere when he was an old man?

Tyrone Huggins (10)
Glenbrook Junior School

The Beautiful Mermaid

Once upon a time lived a mermaid called Africarn. It all started with a man named Jim. There was a little park where Jim sat down. He saw a corner shop so he bought a magazine in which he saw a picture of a beautiful mermaid. The caption read, 'If you want to see this mermaid, you must guess her name.' Jim's friend Alex saw the picture and saw the beautiful mermaid. Jim said to Alex, 'She's beautiful, we must go and find her.'
Alex replied, 'Don't be silly, it's a cold and rainy night and she's only sixteen.'
But Jim insisted, so the two of them looked everywhere for the beautiful mermaid.

Suddenly Jim heard a beautiful singing voice and he heard someone call, 'Africarn.' He looked and saw little helpers in a big palace full of water. Jim and Alex tried to look smart and they walked into the palace. The beautiful mermaid said, 'Take a seat and have some of my cherry cake.'
Jim took some cake and the mermaid told her helpers to take Jim and lock him up in a room by himself. Alex also got locked up in a room. Alex was shouting for help, but Jim ignored him as he had a nice cup of tea.

When it was dinner time, the mermaid and Jim made two portions of macaroni cheese with ice cream for dessert. Over dinner, Jim called the mermaid Africarn and she was so happy, she fell instantly in love with him. Together, they put Alex in the ice cube room, whilst they lived happily ever after.

Rea Nwigwe (10)
Glenbrook Junior School

THE HORROR

Once upon a time, there were two boys at school. They were staring at me, so I walked to a house, then these people moved out. When they went, I went inside. It was dark. I went in every room, then I heard my mum calling me. I waited for my mum to go inside, then I went to my house. My mum said, 'Dinner time.' *Ring, ring.* My mum said, 'Get the phone.'
'Hello?' It was my friend. I said, 'I will meet you at three o'clock.'
'OK.' He said.
So I ate my dinner, then met my friend at three o'clock. I said, 'Let's go inside, it is horrid.'
My friend said, 'Yeah, right.'
Then I said, 'Have a look for yourself.'

My friend Tom and I went in every room. We saw a mirror, Tom went closer, someone was speaking to him, so we both ran out of the house. Tom said, 'You're right, it is horrid.'
'Let's go to my house to see if you're allowed to stay the night.'
Tom said, 'OK.'
I asked my mum and she said yes, so I went to the haunted house. Someone was walking to the door, I was getting scared. I ran out of the house and told my friend James. He said, 'Fibber!' and they never believed me again.

Anthony Street (10)
Glenbrook Junior School

THE DISCO

Katy was waking up one morning. She got out her cereal and milk, she poured the milk in the cereal and started to eat. Then she looked at the clock. It was 7:15. She left the bowl of cereal. She got changed, then she left the house. She got in her car and drove off. She reached the disco, she took off her coat and danced. Katy was tired and she had sausages and salad. Then Katy drank some punch. Katy put on her coat, then got in her car and drove off. She got home and ate supper. Katy got changed, then went to bed and dreamed about a disco.

Kemi Olukoga (10)
Glenbrook Junior School

The Mummy's Tomb

Long, long ago in Egypt there lived a boy called Sam. He was riding a camel in the desert, there were other people with him. There was his mum and dad and there was his dad's friend, the Egyptian. They were discovering pyramids in Egypt. The climbed the big pyramid. All the sand went into their eyes. They climbed until half an hour later when they were at the top of the big pyramid.
'Wow! Look Mum, you can see miles from here!' shouted Sam. Suddenly he dropped down a big hole. 'Ahhh, help me! Help me!' shouted Sam.
'We're coming!' screamed his mum.
Then they went down a rope. 'Come on, let's see if there is a mummy in here,' said Sam.
So they looked around. There were cobwebs and insects. His mum jumped up and said, 'I want to get out from here, now!' Just then, there was the sound of thunder. The stones in the pyramid were tumbling down. They tried to get out. Sam's dad's friend was acting strange, he would not get out of the pyramid.
They all shouted, 'Come on, come on!'
'I can't,' he mumbled. He stood there until the last minute, when he changed his mind. 'Get me out!' But the hole closed and they never saw or heard of him again.

Sanna Khan (10)
Glenbrook Junior School

FOOTBALL PREMIERSHIP DISASTER

In a big, wide city called Thorn City, everybody was crazy about football, except Frederick Black. He hated football because everywhere would be crowded and noisy. Thorn City's stadium was five yards from Frederick's house, so when matches were at home for Thorn City, he had to hide underneath his pillow. Frederick was a tall man with brown, spiky hair and blue eyes, with brown glasses. Normally he would wear a grey top and black trousers. Thorn City every year would come second place out of the four teams. The team that always won was Sunshine City. Sunshine City was unstoppable, every match they won. The team that they faced in all of their matches, the opponents would not score one goal. The 2002 Premiership began, it was Thorn City versus Spring Town. Frederick was at home trying to think of an evil plan that would spoil Thorn City's final match. Skilful Steven was running down the wing then he crossed the ball to Clumsy Colin, who miss-headed the ball, then Jumping Jerome scored. It was 1-0 to Thorn City. The team was congratulating Clumsy Colin because his miss-header fooled the goalkeeper. Spring Town kicked off. They started to take long shots, but Handy Herbert made a brilliant save. After a while, Brilliant Brian scored to make it 2-0. It was half-time. The commentator said, 'Sunshine City are winning 4-0 against Eastwood Town.' The scores stayed the same at full time.

The next match was Thorn City versus Eastwood Town. The match began and in 45 seconds, Eastwood Town had scored. Then Handy Herbert booted the ball so far, then Clumsy Colin controlled the ball, then swung his foot. It missed the ball, then the Eastwood defender sprinted past everyone and scored a goal. It was half-time. 'It is 2-0 here, but with Sunshine City against Spring Town, the scores are 7-0.' Thorn City scored when the match began, then they scored again. Then it was a penalty. Clumsy Colin took it. He scored, then it was full time. 'The tables look like this:

	Played	Goal	Points
Sunshine City	2	+11	6
Thorn City	2	+3	6
Eastwood Town	2	-2	0
Spring Town	2	-9	0

Sunshine City are in the lead because of goal difference.'

It was the final and if it is a draw, Sunshine City will win the cup. It stayed 0-0 till the 89th minute, when Thorn City got a free kick. Brilliant Brian scored. It was time to give the trophy, but Frederick Black was running off with it. The cops caught him and the trophy was handed over.

Brian Blackwood (10)
Glenbrook Junior School

THE SPIDER WEB AND THE HAUNTED HOUSE

One day in a dark, dark, haunted house, there lived an old woman called Shelly. She loved spiders, so one day, she collected spiders in a box. The spiders made a big web. A year later, Shelly went back there and there were dozens of them. When Shelly went to bed, she heard someone downstairs. Shelly crept downstairs still half asleep and she said, 'Hello! Who are you? I want you to get out of my house now!' She was phoning someone, but the line was cut off. In the morning, Shelly was out in the garden doing some gardening, planting some potatoes and flowers. On 13th July 1989, Shelly moved to a haunted house, but she didn't know about it. By now, Shelly was eighty-four years old and she liked the haunted house and spiders. She lived in the countryside, she had grandchildren who were 10 - 14 years old. She had a husband, but he died at ninety-four years of age. One evening, he had taken her out to the ball and two nights after, he had a heart attack and died. It was very upsetting. He died in her house and they were there for twenty-seven years. He bought her a chain with a love heart with purple diamonds and normal diamonds in it, and it was real and it shone. Shelly wore it all the time.

One morning, she went down to the market and got some apples, oranges and vegetables. When she got home, she made an apple pie because her grandchildren were coming down, and they loved apple pies. Shelly went to the shop and bought some chocolate to make some chocolate cakes. When they came, they brought her some presents and the lived happily ever after.

Joanne Wallace (10)
Glenbrook Junior School

FRIENDSHIP

Paula had long, blonde hair and a neat do. It was her first day at Chipfly School. She already had girls queuing to be her friend because of her posh, rich look. Paula was spoilt for choice. She didn't know whether to be Nia's friend or Leanne's friend. By play time, Paula had half the girls in the school wanting to be her friend. Paula was quite pleased with herself, as she had never been this popular at any of her other schools.

'Right,' said Nia one sunny play time. 'Who do you want to play with, me or all these other people?'

Paula stared around at the girls queuing to be her friend. There were kind-looking girls, mean-looking girls, popular-looking girls and unpopular-looking girls. After minutes of looking, Paula decided to be friends with a girl who looked the complete opposite of herself, the girl was called Malina and had big glasses, orange hair and clothes that were old and ragged.

Malina and Paula were friends for years and years and still to this day, People who go to Jumbo Graveside, where Malina and Paula are buried, will see a poem that says:

> *'Malina and Paula,*
> *Wherever they shall be,*
> *Are great friends forever,*
> *Even though we cannot see.'*

Aisha Green (10)
Glenbrook Junior School

AN AMAZING DISCOVERY

I looked up and there before me, I saw a golden axe with a warning engraved on the blade in blood-red rubies. At first I was excited and then scared, rubies were my birthstone. The warning read:

> *Rubies are your stone,*
> *March is your birth,*
> *America is your homeland,*
> *Today will get much worse.*

Then, anxious and scared, I ran as fast as I could, but no matter how much I tried, I couldn't change direction so I stopped. The axe was nowhere in sight, I was alone in darkness. I stood there, my heart pounding. I took a big, deep breath, I could see the cold carbon dioxide coming out of my mouth. I turned around and no sooner had I looked up, than the axe was there. It made a dive for my head but I ducked and put my right hand in the air above my face. At first, the axe just stayed there, but then it make a sudden drop. I moved my face, but I kept my arm there. 'Help!' I cried and then I looked down, and on the floor was a great pool of blood. My hand was writing in it . . .

The writing read,

> *I warned you, did I not.*
> *You can't run and you can't hide.*
> *I got rid of your hand,*
> *I'll get rid of your life.*

I could have sworn that my heart stopped. Everything around froze, even my breath in mid air. I stood so still that even the blood pouring from my arm stopped moving. All of a sudden, a scab came where my hand was. I screamed, but nothing came out, not even a squeak. My voice had gone, but yet it was there. A single tear rolled down my cheek and it landed in the pool of blood, the writing disappeared, so did my hand and the axe. I dropped to the floor with fear, where was I to go? What was I to do? All these questions were running through my head, but the one I thought about the most was *Is it all a dream?*

All of a sudden, I felt a sharp pain running though my body, up my arm, into my shoulders and down through my legs. It felt like I was dead, but yet I was alive. Then the pain went as quickly as it had come. I heard footsteps drawing nearer and nearer. I jumped to my feet, my arm still hanging at my side, heavy and useless.

I thought I could hear my baby sister crying. (This sister who I hated ever since my mother told me she was pregnant, the sister got my room, my toys, and most importantly, my mum.) Then I saw her crawling towards me. I ran towards her and picked her up with my one working arm. She cried and cried, each small, watery tear landing gently on my fingers. Every time a tear ran down her soft cheek, I grew to love her more and more. As the love I had for her filled my heart, gradually my hand grew back until all that was left was a scar where the axe had cut off my hand.

I looked up and all the scenery around me had changed. I was back home, rocking my little sister to sleep, my arm was in a sling. I looked into the eyes of my little sister and asked her, 'Do you remember?' then she winked at me and fell fast asleep.

Niyonu Agana-Burke (10)
Glenbrook Junior School

SCARE YOURSELF TO SLEEP

When my cousin comes to stay, we sleep in a tent at the bottom of the garden. We don't let my brother in, he'd spoil everything. We love it, just the two of us lying there side by side talking. We tell each other jokes very quietly, because we don't want anyone to know we're there. We know Simon is there outside the tent trying to listen, so we whisper. We don't want him to spoil everything. Soon it starts to get dark. The shadows rise and outside it grows quiet and still. Then me and my cousin always play the same game. We call it 'Scare yourself to sleep'.
First I whisper to her, 'Are you scared?'
'No,' she says, 'are you?'
'No,' I say, 'but I bet I could scare you.'
'Go on then,' she says.
'Right,' I say and I tell her all about the Dustbin Demons. They are the gangs of evil little goblins who live under the rubbish in the bottom of dustbins. Each night, just as the moon comes up, they throw back the dustbin lid with a clatter, ready to go on the prowl. They fling all the rotten food up in the air, then out they crawl, climbing over one another in their hurry to be off. They swarm around the garden until they find some helpless creature foolish enough to be out alone. Then they carry it off, struggling and squealing, back to their smelly den, never to be seen again.

She wriggles down into her sleeping bag. I smile to myself, that scared her. Suddenly there is a *crash!* It sounds like a dustbin lid banging and clattering on the garden path. Our hearts are thumping. Then we hear, 'Gotcha, hee, hee, hee!'
'Oh Simon, go away, you are stupid,' we say. 'You didn't scare us.' But we move our sleeping bags a little closer together. Next, she tells me about the flying cat. It creeps along on its soft padded paws, pretending to be an ordinary cat, but at the stroke of midnight, it sprouts wings and flies up into the air, a giant furry moth that miaows.
'Never sleep with your tent open,' she warns me, 'because when the flying cat finds its prey, it swoops down and lands on it. It sinks its claws and its razor-sharp teeth into its victim and sucks its blood. Slurp, slurp, slurp.' We both shiver and hold hands. She doesn't like cats, I don't like moths.

Just then, something blunders into the tent, flapping its wings. 'Miaow, miaow, slurp,' it says.
'Look, Simon,' we say, 'just go away will you. You aren't funny.' We lie there quiet for a moment, ignoring him. At last I say, 'That's nothing. Wait until you hear about the tree creeper. It's like a huge brown stick insect which climbs from tree to tree. It hugs the branches, waiting to drop down on anyone who walks underneath. Never pitch your tent under a tree,' I warn her, 'because if you do, in the middle of the night, the tree creeper will drop down and crawl inside and crush you in its stick-like arms. Crunch! Crunch!' Neither of us likes that story. I don't know where I got such a horrid idea from. We reach out and hold hands. Suddenly, there is a *bang!* as if half a tree has landed on top of the tent. We scream and hide our eyes. We hear 'crunch, crunch, crunch,' then a silly laugh! 'Simon, you are stupid!' we say, 'You spoil everything. Go away!'

Now my cousin is very quiet. I begin to think perhaps I have won, but then she says, 'You don't know about the Invisible Man do you? He can walk through walls and see through doors. He could pass through this tent like a beam of light. He could be standing there by your side and you wouldn't even see him. You'd just feel him breathing on you. It doesn't matter where you pitch your tent,' she tells me, 'the Invisible Man would get you. Nothing could keep him out.'
Now it is really dark. There isn't a sound, I am lying here wide awake. I grab my cousin's arm. 'What does he do,' I say, 'if he gets you?'
She yawns. 'He dissolves you,' she says, 'so you're invisible too.'
'And then what?'
There is no answer.
'Then what happens?'
But my cousin has gone to sleep. I can hear her breathing through her mouth as if she has a peg on her nose. Now I start to hear other sounds. It's raining, hitting the tent, tap, tap, tap. But I begin to think it's the Invisible Man's footsteps. He's coming to get me. Tap, tap, tap, tap. Then I hear the wind blowing against the tent, but I think it is the Invisible Man, breathing heavily, panting as he comes closer, ready to dissolve me. I slide down into my sleeping bag and hide. Now I can hear a ripping sound. Someone is trying to get in. I reach for my torch

and switch it on in time to see the zip burst open and a horrible face appear in the gap.

'Can I come in?' says Simon, 'It's raining out here and I'm getting wet.'
'Oh, Simon, you are stupid,' I say, but I won't send him away. He slides down between me and my cousin and we start to giggle. Then I remember the picnic we brought with us. 'Are you hungry?' I say. Simon grins. We sit up in the torchlight, side by side, just the two of us eating our midnight feast. We whisper so we don't wake my cousin. That would spoil everything.

In the morning, when she asks me who ate her food I tell her it was the goblins.
She said, 'But I don't believe in goblins.'
Even so, I told a story about goblins.

Kristina Madden (10)
Glenbrook Junior School

WHAT LIES BENEATH

Once upon a time in the deep under sea, where the fishes are nowhere to be seen, there lies a powerful force. Now that force forever lives in one creature. A danger known to man, it looks like a dinosaur. It swims like an eel, flies like a bird, it erupts like a volcano. No, we don't speak his name, but we call it triceratops.

'One of these days, the beast will return to our village and try to eat us,' said the wrinkly old man called Jedi, the best food seller in the world. Suddenly, triceratops appeared.

Calvin Johnson (10)
Glenbrook Junior School

THE HAUNTED SCHOOL

Jack was a Year 5. They had to demolish his school because it was crumbling to bits. Jack's mum knew that the school was getting demolished and she had a school in store for him. The school was called 'The School of Weird Science'.

The story starts here

Jack was not happy when he found out his one and only school was getting demolished. He only thought about his friends for the last ten minutes.

Jack went to his mum and said, 'What about school?'
Mum replied, 'I've got a school in-store for you.'

When Jack woke up the next morning he got ready and went to see what his first day of school was like.

The school was an old time school. He walked through the corridor and a spear went for his head, but missed.

He got to his classroom. There were student skeletons everywhere. There was a loud bang. A bullet glided through is hand. He looked around to see his worst nightmare . . .

To be continued . . .

Denton De Frietas (10)
Glenbrook Junior School

THE SPIES AT THE DISCO

One day in a land far, far away there was an agent called Bad and an agent called Good. A girl called Mary was walking by and in her hand was an invitation to a disco. On the girl's neck was a diamond necklace. Agent Bad tried to get the necklace but Mary was too fast for him. Agent Good was trying to stop Agent Bad from getting the diamond.

Finally, it was the disco. Everyone in the land was there and Agent Good and Agent Bad were there too. Mary was talking to her friend when Agent Bad crept up to her and shouted out, 'I have the diamond necklace!' Mary was shocked. Agent Bad threw it up in the air and Agent Good caught it. Agent Good quickly ran out. Standing next to the door was Agent Bad. He snatched the diamond necklace off Agent Good and went back to the lab and out the diamond on the clip. He pressed the button and he became the most powerful man in the world.

Kori Hendrickson (9)
Glenbrook Junior School

THE CROW

Once there was a crow who was supposed to have a legend, which was when someone dies the crow will bring them back to life to set things straight.

One day my father died shortly after the legend was made. My father died because a man called James poisoned him when he was twenty-one. His life was all very happy until then. Two days later I thought I saw him, then I saw a crow on his shoulder. I asked him what his name was.
He said, 'The Crow.'
I turned around to say I don't believe you, but he was gone. I ran for two hours looking for The Crow. I went home to have a real English breakfast - eggs, bacon, sausage, fried bread and a big cup of tea. Then exactly the same crow jumped on the window sill. I said, 'Go away, you gut slackin pig.'

Then the man who called himself 'The Crow' appeared. He said, 'Where is your mum?'
'Out,' I replied and then said, 'do you want a drink?'

When I finished he was gone - I hate it when he does that. The crow went to find James. He found him twenty-four hours later. He shouted, 'Poison vine.' It touched his arm and he died straight away. The crow went to rest in peace for all his life and died.

Luke Bradbury (10)
Glenbrook Junior School

SCARY SPIES

Dianna was a most ordinary young girl. She was mixed race and had lovely long black hair. She was very tall, slim and very pretty. She lived in her school as it was a boarding school. Dianna was what you might call a perfectly ordinary eighteen year old girl. Except for one thing - she was a spy!

Unlike most spies you would have heard of, Dianna was a spy on her own. Dianna was not the type of girl you get upset easily or be unkind. All of a sudden, a teacher came out and gave her a letter, very important apparently. As Dianna opened the letter she noticed the funny green computer writing and knew straight away who it was from. It was from Max, her boss. He was very kind, not just because he depended on Dianna to save the world. Dianna was not very happy when she read the letter. It said:

Dear Dianna,

Please go to the car park now and get into the white limo.

Five minutes later Dianna was driving in the limo. She was down underneath the limo, as it was no ordinary limo. Dianna had worked her way down into a building under the seat. She walked down a corridor with no windows and no doors. Someone was coming towards her. She was trapped, what would she do? Stay tuned for next week's edition of Scary Spies.

Mabina Beccari (10)
Glenbrook Junior School

JOHNNY'S GOT MAGICAL POWERS

Meet Johnny. Johnny's mum, dad, grandpa and grandma. Now I've got that sorted I can start with the story. Oh, I forgot to tell you, I used to be Johnny's guardian angel, Emaily - well, that was Johnny's guardian angel. Anyway, let me get on with the story.

It all started when we were on a camping trip. Of course, I was there but his parents couldn't see me! So we were on this camping trip, Johnny was up to mischief as always. Johnny's mum told Johnny to go and play while they were setting up the camp, so I went off with him.

We were running around when Johnny spotted a man wearing a brown grass skirt. I started to giggle, but Johnny walked up to the man and said, 'What are you doing here?' in his politest voice.

The man got mad and shouted, 'Emotep told me to give the first person to talk to me these powers so I shall give you the powers!'

Johnny didn't understand a word but I did. I told Johnny to run, run as fast as he could but it was too late. The man had already got his wand and swish, the magic had already got Johnny.

Before the man left he said, 'Emotep has given you his powers and treat them with care. If you say goodbye and then somebody's name, the next day they will be gone. And with that a flash and a big bang and he had gone.

When we were walking back I told Johnny about the powers that the man had given him. Of course Johnny could not understand a word he was saying. He wanted me to tell him again and again because he couldn't believe it.

The next day, when they got home, Johnny was so tired he went to sleep. When his grandparents went home Johnny said, 'Goodbye Grandma, goodbye Grandpa,' and guess what? The next day his grandparent's died.

Mum was in a right state, and so was Dad. I told Johnny what he had done and he said he had forgot. I told him to be more careful and he said he would.

The next morning Johnny's dad left for work. Johnny said, 'Goodbye Dad,' and then he remembered and he ran up to his dad and said, 'Dad, don't go!'
'I have to go to work Johnny,' replied Dad and off he went.

When the milkman came round that day he said, 'Hello.' But as he was walking out of the gate he fell. Mum ran to see if he was all right but he wasn't, he'd died!

Why did the milkman die and not Dad?
Because Dad *was* the milkman.

That evening the man with the brown grass skirt came and shouted with envy, 'You have betrayed the powers of Emotep badly. You shall be punished and your punishment will be *death!*'

'No! No!' screamed Johnny. I tried to stop the man but he had already got Johnny.

Daisy San (10)
Glenbrook Junior School

Mysterious House

Once upon a time there were five girls called Aisha, Elizabeth, Mabina, Niyonu and Shenekia.

Elizabeth thought that they should go out some time and they all said yes. So they decided to go on a Friday after school. They walked down the street and saw a house, which looked like a posh one. They went up the path and into the house. It looked creepy inside. There were cobwebs.
Niyonu said, 'Let's get out.'
The door slammed and it was locked. They all started to scream very loud. Then a skeleton fell from out of nowhere. They started to scream again and ran up the stairs while screaming. They saw a door and it said on it 'bedroom'. They went in and they all said 'Wow!' because it looked very posh. They saw a butler who came and gave them a drink. Because this house was very mysterious and strange they could not believe it. It was like posh and haunted together - one bit was posh and the other was haunted, which they all thought strange as they didn't know if they were going in a posh bit or haunted bit.

Well, the girls were going to sleep there.
Niyonu said, 'I want to stay here but don't know if we are going in a posh bit again.'
So they had a sleep where they were.

In the morning they moved on and came to another door saying 'living room'. They opened the door and it was so haunted. They wanted to run down the stairs and get out of the house, but they were in the middle of the room and the door was shut tight. They could not get out but they saw a door that did not have a sign on it.
Shenekia said, 'I'm going to open this door.'
Something jumped out as the door opened and they all ran down the stairs. They ran out the door and down the street, around the corner into Niyonu's house.
Niyonu's mum said, 'What is the matter?'

They said, 'Phone our mums to come and get us please!'
Mabina said, 'It's a long story.'

They all went home and explained it to their parents. They said, 'Why did we go out anyway?' They all decided not to go out, only to their own houses and have fun. And they all lived happily ever after.

Elizabeth Muir (10)
Glenbrook Junior School

THE MAGIC KEY

Don't ever try a key for everything!

Once upon a time there was a big girl called Amy. It was her 10th birthday and she had lots of fun. Amy had lots of presents. She got a puppy dog, a diary and a skipping rope. When everyone went she forgot one special present from her best auntie. When Amy opened it, it was something very strange. 'Wow!' shouted Amy. Amy read the card that her auntie gave her. 'Dear Amy, how are you? I've missed you. This key that I've given you is personal. It is really powerful, but I warn you, it's dangerous.' Amy was surprised. There was another present. She opened it and there was a magical small ballerina. Amy put the key on the ballerina's back. When she took the key out, the ballerina twisted round. Then there was a song with it. 'Close your eyes, say your name'. Amy did not understand what it meant. 'This is junk,' said Amy. Amy tried the key on her diary but when she put the key in, it started to hit her head. 'Ow!' shouted Amy. 'Now I know why I have used the key for the ballerina.' So Amy put the key back in and followed the instructions.

Once she did as instructed, everything started getting clean. Amy was so surprised she wrote a letter back to her auntie. When her auntie wrote back she said that she never knew Amy was surprised. When it was night the ballerina started walking. Something was strange, but Amy did not know . . .

Tayo Oke (8)
Glenbrook Junior School

THE SPOOKY CASTLE

Once upon a time there were two boys called Mark and Shamir. They went camping in the woods with their tents. They found a good place to sleep for the night. Just then, behind the bushes, there was a big castle. The two boys went inside to see what it was like. Inside they went into a room and saw a dead body. They ran out of the room and into another. In that room there were heads on ropes and big knives. A man was chopping off the heads and he started to chase the boys round the castle. He said, 'If I catch you, it will be your heads next.'

They ran into the sitting room and out of the castle. They packed up their tents and ran home.

Mark Buchanan (9)
Glenbrook Junior School

THE BOX OF RICHES

It was my birthday. The place was packed and I was sweating. I cut the birthday cake - it was a chocolate cake with Smarties and M & Ms on. After a while, it was time to open my presents. First I opened a flat box. It was a training session with France, England and Spain. It was a once in a lifetime opportunity but it wasn't even the best present of the night. I picked up an old dusty box. I opened it. I was amazed at what I saw. I ran up the stairs and put it under my bed. After the party was over I went to bed.

I was playing football with my friends when I remembered that I had the box. I was just about to open my mouth when Kayonn said to me, 'That party was heavy, wasn't it?'
'Yeah, yeah, but wait, I've got something to show you.'

They were amazed, just like I was the other night.

We went to a TV company. The employer said to us, 'What are you kids doing here? You're too poor, what are you going to pay with, gold?'
'Yeah!'

The piece of gold went flying out of my hand. Now we have our own television programme called The Kid's Planet.

Akin Anderson (9)
Glenbrook Junior School

SPOOK HALL

Once upon a time there was a haunted house. An old woman named Mrs Potter lived there. One stormy night a ghost appeared with an axe. Quietly he crept up behind Mrs Potter, as she was watching television. The ghost sliced Mrs Potter in half, her blood squirted into the air. She was dead! The police found her body. They locked up the house forever. The police told everyone never to go into the house.

Four years later a family bought the house. Their names were Mr and Mrs Hassan. They had a daughter named Emily who was nine years old. One night Emily was sleeping when suddenly the ghost reappeared. He held the axe in his hand. Emily woke up, she looked at her bedroom clock and the time was 5.30am. She saw the ghost and let out a scream. She jumped out of bed and ran. A voice was telling her to run outside. Emily ran towards the back door and burst out into the garden. The ghost followed. All of a sudden the sun rose over the trees. Emily heard a horrible noise from behind. As she turned around she saw the ghost melting away. He was never seen again!

Samson Abayomi (9)
Glenbrook Junior School

WICKED STEPMOTHER

Once there was a girl called Olivia. She was eight years old. She really liked the latest boy band Roccaworms. She had a stepmother who always made her do all the cleaning. Her father had died so she had to live with her wicked, old, mean stepmother.

Her stepmother boasted that she was the best at singing and used to be in a girl band called Pooches. The next day there was news that Roccaworms were having a tour in London. When Olivia heard the news she started screaming and asking her stepmother if she could go to the tour.
Her stepmother said, 'Only if you clean the entire house, including the garden and garage.'

The next day was the tour. Olivia woke up early and started cleaning. She finished at eight o'clock.
A strange man appeared and asked her, 'Do you really want to go to the tour?'
She replied, 'Yes I really do.'
Then the man said, 'Here is a dress and make-up. You shall go because it's me, your dad in spirit.'

So she went. They performed brilliantly. One of the members saw Olivia and married her. She lived with him in a mansion.

Nana Frimpong (9)
Glenbrook Junior School

THE EVIL MONKEY

Yesterday Billy got an evil monkey. When he took it home it threatened him that it would kill him and the world, because he wanted to take over the world.

On Monday the monkey killed a cop, Billy's best friend, his mum and his teacher. Two days later Billy's whole class was dead.

It was so obvious but Billy knew it seemed crazy. He told the police but they just laughed and put him in a mad home.

The monkey killed the police. It was not long till it tracked down Billy.

It killed the guards and opened the door . . . there was a scream. The monkey had a ballpoint pen with Billy's eye on it as a warning.

After the monkey chopped off Billy's eye to keep it as a trophy. It was chaos, madness and frightening.

After Billy's last attempt, it killed Billy.

Two years later . . .

The monkey took over the world.

Nicholas Marongwe (10)
Glenbrook Junior School

TRIP BANBUSSAL IN LOST GALAXY

One day in a little house there was a team of six kids. Their names were Tamara, Tomiwa, Kai, Osimo, Ayo and Sodiq. They were practising their new song. The song goes like this, 'Say hey hey, trip bam, we're the team with attitude. Trip bam.' Their song was a hit.

One day they were playing in the playground when a spaceship hit the ground. They did not notice when a long ladder came out but nothing came out of the spaceship. The kids accidentally went into the spaceship and the spaceship automatically took off into space and dropped them in space.
Tomiwa said, 'Where are we?'
Kai said, 'By my calculations, I will say we are in space.'

A meteor took him for a ride round space, what a terrible ride it was. Ayo was laughing so hard that he hit a planet. The team were laughing. The team went up to see what Ayo had hit. It was planet Mars. 'That will explain why you have such a big lump on your head,' they all said.
'Very funny,' said Ayo.

Osimo pointed at a hole containing fire. The team jumped over the hole, except Tomiwa. He said, 'If you can jump over the fire, then so can I.' When he jumped he landed right in the fire. His bottom was red-hot.
Tomiwa said, 'I win.'
The team laughed at Tomiwa's stunt.
'No more, thank you,' said Tomiwa.
'Hey, where is Osimo?' Tamara said.
'I don't know,' they all said.

Sodiq picked up a letter and said, 'Look over here.'

Ayo read the letter saying, *if you wish to see Osimo come to the last house you see because I am holding him hostage. From Chumpleon.*

Ayo said, 'The last house! Where is that going to be?'
Tomiwa and Kai said, 'We have no idea. Beats us.'

The team went halfway and started to sing, 'When you're in the deepest holes, when you're in the darkest pits and you're on the verge on the edge to call it quits, there could be a big day just there for you, a hip hip hooray for you, and it's just along the way so hang in small kid, hang in.'

After that they found the house and Chumpleon had found his four henchmen.
The leader said, 'Get them!'
Ayo said, 'We knew you would say that, split up team.'

Tomiwa and Kai jumped over a table, bent down and tripped over the two baddies that were chasing them. Tomiwa said, 'Give me five Kai!'

Upstairs Ayo jumped on the wall, did a back flip and a spin headstand and when he did his spin headstand he kicked two baddies as well.
Chumpleon said, 'Come on you lot, let's go. This place is set to blow in twenty seconds.'
Tomiwa said, 'Anyone up for leaving?'

The team ran out straight away. The team took a shortcut and went ahead of the crooks. They made a trap right near a cliff. The trap was noodles.
Ayo said, 'Get your noodles while they're hot!'
Chumpleon slipped into the noodles and fell of the cliff.
Ayo said, 'Hey, I'll just put it on your tab.'
At the bottom there was a net that caught Chumpleon and his henchmen. Sodiq and Tamara untied Osimo and told the team they should go. The team carried the five crooks into their new spaceship and took off. They began to sing, 'Oh, oh what a day to remember. I remember it just that way. I will never forget to remember that day.'

Ayo Unoarumhi (10)
Glenbrook Junior School

THE FORBIDDEN HOUSE

My father pulled up and I jumped out holding my friend's birthday present. He drove off, leaving me to find the house. A cold breeze caused the leaves to erupt. I seemed to remember her house being number seventeen. I scampered up the path and tried the doorbell, but it didn't seem to work. I glanced upwards at the house which was strangled in ivy. I could see nothing through the dusty windowpanes, so I pushed the rusty door handle. To my amazement it opened, so I tiptoed in.

Dust lay thick and undisturbed. There were moth-eaten sofas and wormy cupboards. This couldn't be my friend's house. I turned to go, but the doors slammed and stuck. I scurried up the gloomy steps in search of escape and entered a small room. Thankfully, there was a window, but the locks had rusted and wouldn't open. On the ground lay a large, heavy walking stick with which I smashed the window. I climbed through the frame and down the ivy to safety.

When I looked back from the street, there seemed to be a shape at the broken window and the faint sound of laughter in the wind . . .

Natasha Sheppard (9)
Grange Park Prep School

THE DAY I DEALT WITH THE BULLY

I was trying to find my missing pencil case. 'Miss, someone's taken my pencils,' I complained.
Miss Hammers sighed. 'Has anyone got Ellie's pencils?' she asked.
Steven, the bully, raised one hand, the other rummaging in his desk.
'I have, Miss,' he said with an evil grin on his face.

The next lesson was PE, but where was my PE bag? Again I said, 'Miss, I can't find my PE kit.'
'Can't you see I am a bit too busy to help you again!' she snapped nastily.
I just had to miss the lesson.

At home time, Steven appeared. 'Oh, look what I've found,' he said and handed over my PE bag. Obviously, Steven was taking my stuff.

The next day there were exams and the first was spellings, but Steven had taken my book. I was not going to tell Miss Hammers. I searched the cloakroom, then as I walked back to class without my book, I bumped into my friend. 'Here's your book, Ellie. I saw Steven hide it,' she explained.
I marched up to the teacher's desk and told her the truth.
'Steven, you will have detention for three days!' she shouted.
Steven was never horrible to me again.

Leanne Kean (8)
Grange Park Prep School

TIME TRAVELLER

It all started one Sunday. I was walking down my highly modern street when all of a sudden, everything became old fashioned. This was very weird. My own house was Victorian, then I noticed the people's clothes and my clothes were old fashioned.

I ran inside. The wallpaper, my bed, the picture of the queen, they'd all changed to Victorian style. I ran outside. 'What year is it?' I asked an odd looking man.
He replied, '1850, Madam.'
I must have travelled back in time!

There was a big crowd in the main square. Queen Victoria was there, she was inviting people up to perform in a talent show. She pointed at me and suddenly, I knew I was singing in front of everyone and was named the winner.

I went back home, jumping for joy. 'Mum, Dad,' I announced, swinging the door open. My mother was crying and my father had his hand on her shoulder. The police were there. 'What's going on?' I asked.
'You've been gone for over a day,' she yelled, running and putting her arms around me.

Later on, I explained where I had been. My mother shook her head and said, 'Your imagination!'

Victoria Ware (9)
Grange Park Prep School

THE ADVENTURES OF CREAMY AND STAR

One boiling hot day, Creamy and Star were in their run when Tortoise, the neighbourhood cat, tipped the run up! 'Eeek!' cried Star.
'Earthquake! Earthquake!'
'Silly,' squeaked Creamy. 'It's Tortoise, the cat!'
'Yeah, come to eat us,' said Star, crossly.
'Look!' Creamy spotted the paddling pool and scampered towards it.
'Fancy a swim, Star?'
'Yes! How do we get in?' puzzled Star.
'Look in the playhouse.'

Creamy walked in and came out with a guinea pig sized ladder in her mouth. They got into the pool and swam about. Then up came their friends Duke, Lettuce, Dandy and Lion. 'Fancy a swim, guys?' Creamy asked.
'Yes! Let's play races. Whoever wins gets a quarter of everybody's carrot!' exclaimed Dandy.
'Everybody in a line!' instructed Star. 'Ready, steady, go . . . Duke's in first place, followed by Creamy and Lion, Dandy and Lettuce a few inches from the starting line,' commentated Star. 'And the winner is . . . Lion!'

That evening, when Star and Creamy were eating three quarters of a carrot each, Star said to Creamy, 'I think I'm getting the hang of piggy-paddle.'
'Why didn't you join in the races?' questioned Creamy.
'Cos you needed a commentator,' answered Star.

Emily Ross (8)
Grange Park Prep School

GHOST!

I was lying in bed, trembling as if I was a rattle in a baby's hand. Strange noises made me even worse. I heard quiet creaking on the staircase. It got louder and louder, so I knew someone was coming upstairs.

Suddenly there was a loud banging, a dreadful yelling, the windows rattled, the raging wind whistled louder than ever. I jumped under the bed, scared to death.

There was a sudden bang and everything was quiet again. A bright light shone out from under the bed. All of a sudden, something caught my eye, almost like I was being hypnotised.
'Save yourself before it's too late!' a ghost chanted over and over again.
'Save myself? What do you mean?' I was confused.
'I was the first to live in this house when it was built in 1910. One night, on April the 4th my husband and I were lying in bed. Next door, our daughter Naomi was crouched up in a little ball under the cover.'
'Wait!' I interrupted, 'My name is . . .'
'I know your name, Naomi. Anyway, you have to get out of here. Every 4th of April, a fire is set. Aaah! It's here!'

Lydia Mills (8)
Grange Park Prep School

A Scary Roller Coaster Ride

I was thrilled with excitement, tense, waiting for the ride to begin. I knew I would regret it. The cart slowly trundled and gradually got faster. Then it slowed down a bit, I was confused as to why. The cart stuttered back. We were rising. We got to the top, my heart skipped a beat and then made up for it.

'Ahhhhhhh!' I screamed, scared out of my wits. The cart of the roller coaster sped down the highest slope, with a solid brick wall staring back. We were about to crash, when the cart jerked harshly to the side and bent around the corner. I gasped for air as I just thought my life was going to end there and then!

I went over a few bumps that weren't that bad. I was still in shock, still scared, but the ride was over. I had survived, but to be quite honest, it was the scariest ride I had ever been on.

Rosie Inns (10)
Guardian Angels RC JMI School

THE MAGIC PENCIL

One hot day, I was going to an exam. I had all the things that I needed. Then I heard a zooming noise down the road, so I went outside to see who it was. Guess who it was? My dad, so I said, 'Bye,' to my mum and got in the car. Then we finally got there.

When we arrived at UCS, I saw my friends Jack and Cameron, then I went into the hall to get my tag. I was told I was in Class C, so I made my way to the class. When I went in the class, I sat down and took my coat off and put it on the back of my chair. the teacher handed the exam papers out.

While I was doing it, a boy turned around and immediately as he turned, his pencil went right up in the air and landed on my desk. Then I picked it up and read what it said. It said, 'The Magic Pencil'. Then, as I was about to write with it, it flew away to its owner.

It was time to go home, so I packed up and gave the paper to the teacher. She said, 'You may leave now,' so I left the room and waited for my dad to pick me up.

I went back home and told my mum what had happened. My dad said, 'It's cool, isn't it?'

Oliver Wilkinson (8)
Hampstead Hill Pre-Prep School

THE UNUSUAL DAY

One day, there was a boy called Sam. He was very good at maths. He was happy, he was going to school. He didn't know that he had an unusual day coming up.

Sam's mum took him to school. When he got there, he walked in, but the teacher said, 'You should have come in the back door.'
He walked through the back door. He put his bag away, and blazer, he walked into the classroom, sat down and did his maths. When he had finished, he handed it to the teacher. She corrected it. She handed it back and said, 'This is appalling, Sam!'

He took it back to his seat and looked at it. 'Oh bother! I'll need a wand to correct all this!' He did, but it was still rubbish.
He did it again and the teacher said, 'Sorry, it's time to finish it.'
It was break time, but the teacher said, 'You have to stay in. Now get on with your work, you've been doing this all morning.'

So he did it, but the teacher said it was still wrong and then gave up. When he came back, it was lunchtime. He had had a very unusual day.

William Snell-Mendoza (8)
Hampstead Hill Pre-Prep School

IF I WERE A KING

One morning I woke. It was one o'clock and my slaves weren't awake. I said to myself, where are those twerps? They are not allowed to stay in bed for as long as this. I will kill them when they wake up.

As time went by, they snored and snored and snored. Finally they woke and I said to them, 'You pathetic pair. You are supposed to wake up at one o'clock. Now for your punishment, you will clean the toilets, iron my clothes and never go to a restaurant again.'

So the slaves went to do what I told them to do.

Milton Karamani (7)
Hampstead Hill Pre-Prep School

IF I WERE KING

If I were king, I would make flying cars for 1p. The flying cars would have rocket boosts and they would go under water too.

I would make a space hotel with a gravity machine and a ping-pong table, and it will have an Xbox. The rooms would have DNA machines and the DNA would have to match to enter.

I would make everything free except for the flying cars. I would not allow graffiti to spread all over the town, and if it did, the people doing it would go to jail.

If any other crime was committed, I would catch them and execute them and that would be a great life.

Sebastian Gemes (8)
Hampstead Hill Pre-Prep School

IF I WERE KING

If I were king, I would change the law for people to spray graffiti on their own houses instead of doing it on the railway and on park walls. Otherwise I would put them into jail.

If you want an autograph, just see if the flags are up. Just come and ask for my autograph and I'll give it to you.

I'll give some of my houses to tramps and other lonely people and I will give them a credit card and a card for getting money for themselves from banks.

Tom Wilkinson (8)
Hampstead Hill Pre-Prep School

IF I WERE KING

If I were king, I would let children drive on the road with their miniature, chargeable cars, but they would have to be older than six.

I would have graffiti chambers so they could spray graffiti in their chambers and not on the walls.

I would let people go on skateboards with paintball guns and their feet would be buckled on.

I would only let policemen put people in jail for a good reason.

Archie Wells (8)
Hampstead Hill Pre-Prep School

IF I WERE KING

If I were a king, I would call my mad scientist to try and take over the world. I would make Arsenal win all the cups, and make Ruairi be my servant. I would make Cameron and Johnny bodyguards and tell Cameron and Johnny to shave Ruairi's head.

I'd make people think America is the best country in the world. I'd give everyone money, even the poor and Ruairi at least £200. I'd make people drive without a license and give Ruairi 209 Ferraris. I would tell police to put murderers in a volcano that's about to erupt, and let Archie do whatever he likes. I'd also give everyone a mansion.

Jack Mead (8)
Hampstead Hill Pre-Prep School

IF I WERE KING

If I were king, there would be flying people, including me. The children would teach the teachers. The fridges would be disposed of in a special way, so it wouldn't affect the ozone layer.

Children would control their parents and their parents would pay the bills. The pets you had would fly. There would be no graffiti.

Everyone would be so rich that they couldn't spend half of their money. Each house would have a jacuzzi, swimming pool and pinball machine.

There would be more music and there would be asteroids flying everywhere.

Daniel Walsh (7)
Hampstead Hill Pre-Prep School

KIDNAPPED

It's a summer's morning and of course, Tom Dweedle's playing PlayStation 2. Sarah Dweedle is boasting in her diary and Sam Dweedle is making a new invention.

Their parents were discussing where they would go for the day. They finally agreed and before you knew it, they were out of the house.

By 6pm they were home, only to find that the burglar (that kept coming to this street) had stolen Mum's jewellery, Dad's laptop, Sarah's prize tennis racket, Sam's electronic piano and Tom's PlayStation 2.

'That robber's stolen stuff again!' bellowed Tom.
'What are we going to do?' wailed Mum.
'I know,' said Sam, 'my invention is a crook detector and by morning, I'll know where he is.'

Now the crook was called Crooked Charlie and he heard this and didn't like it one bit. When they were all asleep, he kidnapped Sam and the machine.

In the morning the kids, Sarah and Tom, woke and went to get Sam. They discovered that the burglar had taken him. They wondered where they would find the burglar without the crook detector. Then they found a sheet with a rough estimate of where the crook lived, that Sam must have worked out. Without thinking, they rang the police and told them to go to the house. Then Sarah and Tom did the same thing.

When Sarah, Tom and the police got in the house, they realised Sam had captured Crooked Charlie. Crooked Charlie apologised for what he did, returned the things he'd taken and went to prison for four years!

James Welsh (10)
Larkswood Junior School

THE MAGNIFICENT BOOTS

One day a boy called James, who wasn't very good at football, was training. Dan Richards, the team captain, started making fun of him so James walked away.

As he was walking, he bumped into an old lady who said, 'I see you need a new pair of boots.'
'Yes,' said James.
'Well here are some boots. Do you want them?'
'Yes please!' So James went back to training and he was picked for the team!

That night James realised they were magic boots. A couple of weeks later, they had the final match at White Hart Lane.

The big day came. James and his team were at White Hart Lane, but there was a big problem. James couldn't find the boots. He knew what had happened. Dan Richards had burnt them!

It was too late, the match had started. In the first half, James played really badly and it was almost a repeat in the second half. It was 6-6. James scored at the end of the match. James had scored the Golden Goal.

Then James realised it wasn't the boots that made him good. He was offered a job at Arsenal, but he said, 'Sorry, I'm Tottenham all over!'

Calum Doyle (10)
Larkswood Junior School

The Ghost Footballer

Once there lived a boy named Kris. Kris loved to play football. He was captain of the school football team. His team were not very good, they were bottom of the league. There were only twenty-two days until the cup finals, this fact worried Kris as he really wanted to win.

One Saturday morning as Kris was having breakfast with his family, his mum came up with a brilliant idea. 'Why don't you put an advert on the notice board at school saying 'Players wanted for school football team. Practice is on Wednesday after school?''

There were only five volunteers. One was a ghost . . . so they all gave their names to Kris. The ghost's name was David.

The next day was a Wednesday and Kris saw something peculiar about David's name. Kris only knew one David and that David didn't like football at all. On Wednesday night at football practice Kris saw only four people. But there, sitting in the changing room was David. (Kris saw David because he has second sight.) Kris found that that there was a drink, a special drink, and if you were a ghost it would turn you into a human being. They both went to the science room and got the drink. They turned David into a human being.

The day came for the cup final. Everyone was excited, they played Chase Lane. The match started and after fifteen minutes, it was 2-0. David scored one and Kris scored the other.

It was half-time now and everyone was happy that they were winning. Before they knew it, the final whistle went and it was 5-0 to Kris's team.

They won the trophy, with the help of David, the ghost.

Charlotte Bacuzzi (9)
Larkswood Junior School

PSYCHO

There was a man called Calum. Calum had been shot in the head, so now he has got brain damage. There is another man called Bullet Tooth. He was shot six times and still lived. He's been known as a criminal and had been put in prison for seven years for murder.

It was Calum's birthday and people brought him presents. The only present he wanted was an Aussalt Limberdon Swiss Army knife. Bullet Tooth was the one who got him that. He also gave him a letter, but it was half torn. Calum went outside to read it. He thought Bullet Tooth was going to kill him, because the letter said, 'I'm going to get you.' When Calum was outside, his mind flashed back to Bullet Tooth's trial, when he had killed someone. His friend came out and said, 'Come on, you're missing out.' But Calum just walked away.

It soon was night and he was running away down an alley so that Bullet Tooth wouldn't get him. Calum ran down an alleyway, there was a dead end! He was doomed, he didn't know what to do. He tried climbing the wall, but he couldn't. Bullet Tooth said, 'I don't know what you're running away for.'
Calum was petrified. Bullet Tooth gave him the knife. Calum said, 'Why are you giving me this?'
Bullet Tooth said, 'For your birthday.'

Calum thought he was going to kill him, but Bullet Tooth took the letter out of his pocket and showed him it. It said, 'I'm going to get you.' Then he took out the other half, and it said, 'A knife.'

Calum took the knife home and enjoyed the rest of his birthday.

JJ Haynes (10)
Larkswood Junior School

THE EMPTY HOUSE

A young girl called Jenny lived next to an empty house. Once, Jenny went to explore the house. As soon as she went in, the door slammed and locked. She started to hear weird noises. There were two ghosts called Joey and Jake, coming along the corridor, so Jenny ran up the stairs. When she ran in a room, the door closed and locked again. Jake followed her. Luckily, there were two ways out, so Jenny ran as fast as she could out of the back.

Jenny ran downstairs and back to the door and tried to get out of the house, but the door was still locked and Joey was coming! He ran into the kitchen and grabbed a knife and tried to stab Joey, but it didn't work because Joey was already dead. He started to laugh at Jenny.

Jenny's brother Tommy knocked at the door, then the ghosts disappeared and the door unlocked. She ran down the stairs and opened the old door and Tommy said, 'What are you doing here?'

She began to tell him about the ghosts, but he didn't believe her.

Emma Moorhouse (9)
Larkswood Junior School

Trapped

It was an ordinary day on Tunnel Avenue. Charlotte and her brother Jack were walking down their street. Suddenly, they saw a bright light in a dark alley and decided to walk towards it.

Bang! In a flash they disappeared and found themselves in a strange place where everyone looked odd. They saw an unusual looking lady dressed in black and asked her where they were. She did not answer for a while, then told them she had been trapped there for hundreds of years.

They decided they would have to try to find a way to escape, or they would end up trapped for life. They looked everywhere, but could not find one. All of a sudden, they saw a strange mirror that was glowing. They were just about to step in the mirror, when the lady jumped in the way and stopped them. They asked her if she would like to escape with them. The lady said, 'Yes, please,' and they all leapt into the mirror together. They were so pleased to find themselves back in their own time.

Now when Charlotte and Jack see something they don't know about, they keep right away.

Katie Morris (10)
Larkswood Junior School

TRAPPED

It was a cold day at 10,000 feet and a fearless boy called Sammy decided that he was going to take skiing lessons because it had been his dream since he was five years old.

Now that he can ski without adult supervision, it is even more exciting. By the way, Sammy was 11 years old.
His parents said, 'Why don't you take Hoodlum along with you?'
Sammy had decided he would take him anyway, because he could talk. (Oops, I almost forgot to tell you, Hoodlum is a dog!)

Sammy started to get really good and skied away from his coach. He decided to take a short cut through the cave, but as he was skiing through, he came to a dead end so he turned back. Unexpectedly, a huge block of snow fell in front of the entrance. Sammy and Hoodlum were trapped in the cave. Sammy took his skis off and began to cry. After a few minutes, Sammy picked them up and to his surprise, he saw a key. He started pacing the floor, trying to think of an idea.

Suddenly, he thought of the most ingenious plan. Sammy ran to the dead end of the cave and started to look at parts of the wall. He tried to see if any of them looked like doors. Eventually, he found a flap which had a keyhole in it. He tried the key he had found earlier and luckily, it opened a secret door.

Sammy went through the door and thought that something was strange, so he wandered around. After a while, he figured out that he was back where he started.

Sammy thought that was the most exciting skiing trip of his life. Sammy said that if he went back to the ski resort, he would have to go back into the cave, because he wanted to see if a different key would take him somewhere else within the skiing resort. Sammy had never been to a more exciting place.

Emma Mahoney (9)
Larkswood Junior School

HAUNTED!

One day after school, Tim and Tom had detention. As they walked home, Tom suggested stealing something from the haunted house. Tim said, 'I'm not sure if we should. The house is haunted. If you go in, you never come out.'
'It's just a house, don't worry,' said Tom.
'Okay,' muttered Tim.
'Good, now let's go.'

They entered, the door creaked. They walked down the corridor, the front door slammed shut. They were frightened, but they went on. They looked in every room, all were empty.

They found a sign saying, *Danger Beware,* on a trapdoor. They opened it and went down the stairs. Tim thought he heard giggling. They found a room full of gold, only visible through a locked door. Someone whispered, 'Help me . . .'

'Let's turn back,' said Tim, shaking.
'It's just the wind,' said Tom.

They crept on through the basement. The whispering started again, it was getting closer and louder. Right beside them, someone screamed, *'Help me!'*

They ran as fast as they could, out of the house. As they ran, they bumped into their teacher - laughing hard. 'That will teach you!' she said.

They never played up in her class again.

Ben Thompson (10)
Larkswood Junior School

The Wand Master

One day, there was a boy called William. He went to the school library and found a book he was really interested in and asked the librarian if he could borrow it. Every day he read ten or eleven chapters and the more he read, the more he got addicted to it. By the end of the week, he had finished the book.

That night, he remembered that part of the book was based somewhere near him. He dreamed that what he read was true and in the morning, he investigated.

Next morning, William went to where he dreamed of, on the way to school. When he got to the place, he looked around for the Wand Master who was said to be near a big oak tree. The Wand Master was nowhere to be seen, so William decided that he would come back after school.

Finally, school was over. William was anxious to see if the Wand Master was by the old oak tree, but still the Wand Master was nowhere to be seen. That night, before he went to bed he planned out how he was going to see the Wand Master and thought that his plan would not fail. His plan was to go to the old oak tree at night, after he had been tucked in.

He escaped through his bedroom window, onto the roof and down the drainpipe into the back garden and headed towards the forest. His mum looked out of the window because she thought she heard a noise, so he hid in the flowers until she went back to bed.

When he got to the forest, he decided that he would camp in the forest and put up some infrared cameras. We set up a computer which was connected to the cameras and waited.

Finally, after half an hour, something appeared. It was the Wand Master. He rushed out to take a picture of him and then he asked him something he really wanted to know, which was 'Are you real or fake? Can you use your magic powers to make me a better boy?'

The Wand Master did as he was asked.

Jamie Flory (10)
Larkswood Junior School

The Soul Catcher

Once a long time ago, a soul called Jake was messing about in his old creaky castle. Jake had blue eyes and blonde hair.

He was messing about until a puff of smoke appeared. A man came out of the smoke with bulging red eyes and scars on his face.
'I will capture you, Jake,' cackled the madman.
Jake fled, but as quick as lightning, he took out a greeny-gold bottle. Jake tried to move, but couldn't. He was sucked into the bottle.

Jake shouted for help. Nobody heard, but a girl called Emma. She went on, then stopped. She heard him call again. Emma decided to find the person who needed her help. She followed the voice and came to the old, creaky castle. Emma went in and found the madman, but he fled. Emma was curious and followed. She followed him to his laboratory, she went in and looked at the soul-killing machine he had built.

She kicked the madman and as he dropped the bottle, he screamed in pain. He got up and came closer and closer. Emma crawled back, saw an axe, grabbed it and stabbed him in the back twice. He fell to the ground dead.

Eileen Kealey (9)
Larkswood Junior School

THE TICKING PRESENT

It was a sunny day and Mitch was playing out with Lewis and Calum over at the park. Mitchell's mum called him on his mobile to say he had to come home. He was at the top of the road, when a man said, 'Do you live at 9 Mulberry Close?'
'Yeah,' he replied.
'Can you take this parcel?'
'Sure, why not.'
On the parcel, it said, 'To a very special grandson.'

Mitch knew who it was from the moment he touched it. It was from his grandad. He hated this grandad, but he liked the other one because he always talked about when he was in the war and he always gave him pocket money.

He took it to his mum and said, 'Mum! Mum! Look what I got from Grandad!'
'Oh, it's ticking. Don't open it!'
'Why?'
'Because it might be a bomb, that's why. Quick, put it carefully down the back of the garden.'

After a couple of weeks, they got a letter from his grandad asking Mitchell if he had liked the clock that he had sent. Grandad thought it would go with Mitchell's bedroom. Mitchell ran to the bottom of the garden and got the parcel. Then he wrote back to Grandad saying he loved it and that it was hanging on the wall in his bedroom. It was a good thing it was a Tottenham Hotspurs clock because it goes well in a Tottenham Hotspurs bedroom!

Mitchell Williams (10)
Larkswood Junior School

THE DAY THE WRITERS CAME!

Everybody in Lathom School was gripped with excitement. The teachers were going bonkers and the children were jumping up and down. Mrs Tritton, the headteacher, had butterflies in her stomach.

Two grand cars drew to a halt outside Lathom car park. The children screamed with joy. A chauffeur got out of the first car and opened the door for . . . J K Rowling! Another chauffeur stepped out of the second car to open the door for . . . Jacqueline Wilson! Both ladies made their way to enter.

'Good morning, good morning,' Mrs Tritton greeted the two authors in her most polite voice.
'Good morning,' answered J K Rowling in an off-hand voice.

Mrs Tritton carefully led the two novelists through the excited crowd of applauding boys and girls. She led them into the assembly hall. At once, the children followed and fought to get a space in the hall. Mrs Mann cleared her throat for a roar at the children. 'Lathom School!' she snapped in a voice that made the children take cover, 'This is no way to behave when we have visitors. We are very lucky to have these two honourable ladies visit our school, but we don't suddenly lose the plot because of that!'

The children grew silent. After interviewing both authors, the children grew closely attached to Jacqueline Wilson. J K Rowling, who was posh and jealous became even more jealous and left. Jacqueline Wilson, seeing that the children liked her so much, decided to stay for another week.

Janani Paramsorthy (11)
Lathom Junior School

THE WARNING

Martin was playing in the garden from 10 o'clock in the morning. His sister Polly was up in her room, wanting to play on the computer. On the computer screen there was a notice, it said, 'Do not switch on!' Polly did not understand the notice, so she went to the computer to turn it on.

Martin and Polly also had a dog named Barkshaw. Barkshaw had already read the notice and went to tell Polly not to switch the computer on, but it was too late. Polly had already set the computer to work.

There on the screen were great big orange and yellow painted blocks. Immediately, she called Martin up to her room. Martin also knew something was wrong. When he saw the computer screen like that, he was shocked. As soon as he saw the screen, he fell to the ground.

Polly tried as hard as she could to pump Martin's heart, but that was also too late. Martin had sadly passed away. Polly wanted to keep this a secret from her mother. Her mother heard her crying and also went up to Polly's room. When she saw Martin lying on the ground, her face went pale white.

Martin's mother thought to herself how Martin had behaved and taught Polly some good manners. He made her forget all about bad manners. Polly felt sad about her brother. Both Polly and her mother had their heads together, crying.

A week later it was time for them to bury Martin in the ground. They buried the body in the back garden and made sure that no one went near the sculpture (The body of dead Martin).

Samreen Iftikhar (10)
Lathom Junior School

THE MAGIC ALLEY

It all happened in London, when a girl's life was changed. Her name was Emily Wood. She was a clever girl with lovely manners and a kind heart.

One rainy day, Emily decided to go to the library, so she put on her boots, hat and raincoat and off she went.

When she got there, she went to the children's corner. She was just about to pick up a great book called 'Dragon Fire' when suddenly, the ground started to shake and the floor opened! She fell down into the ground and landed with a *bump!* She stood up and looked around. It was a dark, cold, damp tunnel.

She started walking. She kept on walking until she came to a very big and dark room. She felt her way around and bumped into something cold and hard. She turned round and right behind her was a huge stone gargoyle.

Before her very eyes, it changed into a huge, real monster. Emily drew back afraid, and so did the monster. It had huge, googly eyes and a green body with purple spots, and a long tail with spikes on it.
'H-h-hello, h-h-how d-do you d-do?' stammered Emily.
'Finally!' cried the monster. 'Oh thank you! Thank you!'
'Um, excuse me. Who are you?' asked Emily.
'Oh, sorry about that!' said the monster. 'My name is Golisha . . . Golisha Mackuu. What's yours?'
'Emily Wood,' replied Emily. 'How did you get like that?'
'Claws, the dinosaur, put a curse on me. Would you like to help me get out of here?'
'Sure!' cried Emily.

So off they went, walking along the alley. After about five hours, Golisha said, 'Can you hear that?' *Boom!*
'Yes!' cried Emily, 'and it's coming this way!'
'Now I see it, it's Claws!'
'Run for it!' shouted Emily. But it was too late, Claws had grabbed them.

'Look what I've found, Makasha!' growled Claws.
Another dinosaur came round the corner and sneered, 'I know what to do with those little . . .'
'Shut up!' said Claws.
Makasha went over to Claws and bit him. Claws dropped Golisha and Emily and howled in pain. Golisha and Emily ran away as fast as their legs could carry them.

Soon, Claws and Makasha realised they had gone and went after them. They soon caught up with them, but Golisha had disappeared!

What Emily didn't know was that Golisha had magic powers! Then soon enough, Emily arrived back in the library. The door slammed shut, there was a deafening roar and then silence. Emily picked up a key and read, 'To the magic alley'. Emily smiled, put it into her pocket and went off home.

Jimena Meza Mitcher (8)
Lathom Junior School

SURPRISE, SURPRISE!

It was a dark night and Wilma Witch, Veronica Vampire and William Werewolf were thinking of a way to slide into Rose-Mary's house.

Rose-Mary was the woman who lived next door to the monsters. She was a woman who loved children. She lived in a ghostly house and never talked to her neighbours.

About the monsters now. Wilma Witch wore ragged black clothes and had a used broom. Veronica Vampire had skin as white as snow and lips as red as blood. William Werewolf looked human when it was day, but he became a wolf at night.

The monsters were thinking of a way to go into Rose-Mary's house. Wilma jumped. 'I've got an idea! Listen William, you're going to knock at the door and pretend you're a nice dog. Grab her attention while we sneak into the house by the back door. When you hear a whistle, run. Go away. When you hear the door closing, come back. That moment, Rose-Mary will get the surprise of her life,' laughed Wilma.
'OK,' Veronica and William answered.

The next day, everyone was in place. Everybody got ready to surprise Rose-Mary.
'Happy 50th birthday!' they all cried.
Rose-Mary smiled.

Amira Lounis (10)
Lathom Junior School

THE HAUNTED TREE

1,000 years ago in a city called London, there was a famous garden. Three children used to own it. They wouldn't allow anybody to play inside the garden. Their names were Gordon, Oliver and Nigel. These children rescued the garden and now it belongs to them.

One night, they went out to the shops to buy some seeds for the garden. Meanwhile, a boy called Michael, who was a gardener, crept into the gardens and he saw a tree. He went to the tree and he touched it. He rubbed off some dirt and he could see something, it said:

> *'Whoever finds the wooden key*
> *is the chosen one to open me.*
> *You won't find it in the grass or earth,*
> *you have to find my place of birth.'*

Meanwhile, the boys had bought the seeds and they were on their way back. As they walked, they could see light glowing from the garden. They ran and just as they got there, the glowing stopped. The three boys were confused, what was going on? Since they had bought the seeds, they planted them and they threw the packet away. It fell next to Michael. Michael picked it up and found a key. That was the missing key to the tree.

Michael opened the door of the tree and he found a lamp. He rubbed it and he had a wish. He wished to be the cleverest gardener and he was. He got out of the tree and kept the key somewhere safe. Michael went out of the garden and lived as the cleverest gardener.

Juwan Sivathas (9)
Lathom Junior School

GHOST STORY

As I walked up to the door, something murmured in my head. I opened the door, it creaked as I turned the handle and I peeped inside. It was an old house. It was fairly dark inside, but luckily I had a torch. As I turned on the switch, I aimed it in front of me. I stared amazed at the sate of this old house, the old pictures of the people. I looked at the pictures, I didn't even know if anyone existed. Suddenly, there was a creak at the door. I thought someone was coming.

There was something about this house that I wanted to know. Why was it hidden in a place like this? How come no one had found it?

I felt there was something moving around me. There were some stairs leading up but no, I couldn't go up. The door slammed and the windows flew open. I was scared.

I ran tremendously fast. I tried to open the door, but at first it didn't open. I turned round to look. Then the door opened. I ran out, but in panic I dropped my torch. I ran and ran.

Ritika Daswani (11)
North Bridge House School

THE GHOST STORY

I was home alone. The babysitter had popped out for ten minutes, but that was half an hour ago! My bedroom door slammed shut. I jumped up like a chicken, a chill ran down my back. I went to investigate.

Quietly, I put my foot on the stairs. I could see the lights flicking on and off under the bedroom door. My heart was beating loudly. The stairs creaked. I froze and listened. Nothing.

I continued slowly up the stairs. I could hear noises coming from my room. I grabbed my mum's favourite vase as a weapon with one hand, and with the other, reached for the door handle. The hairs on the back of my head twitched. I opened the door to my room and looked around.

It was a shambles, my Dreamcast was playing and the window was open . . . phew! Just as I'd left it. But what were those black footprints on the carpet and why did they lead to the wall?

Suddenly, the lights went out. In the mirror, I could see a pair of green-yellow eyes glaring at me. I started to shake with terror. I could hear a voice saying, 'It's OK Simon, you're just having a dream.' I looked up to see my mum's eyes had turned yellow! It was not over!

Simon Arden (10)
North Bridge House School

THE GHOSTS OF BEACHY HEAD

Lara was an odd girl since the tragic death of her best friend, Ami. One late afternoon, Lara went to visit Ami's grave to talk to her. Soon it was dark and the gates were locked. It started to rain, so Lara ran for shelter in a nearby tomb. It was cold and damp like the man's name, Andy Waters.

A week later, Lara and her family went to Eastbourne. Lara went off on her own. She saw signs for Beachy Head where Ami's body was found. Lara started to run up the steep hill, slipping, but finally reaching the top. There was a man already at the top. Lara took no notice of him and peered over the edge, at the same time looking at the man out of the corner of her eye. *Andy Waters* it said on his badge. Lara thought for a moment, then she looked over the edge again. Ami was there, a ghost Ami though. Lara put out her hands longingly to her.

But then she had a feeling of hands on her shoulders, a push, a scream, another tragic, unknown death. Lara's death . . . silence.

Natalie Mallin (11)
North Bridge House School

A DAY IN THE LIFE OF A KILLER

I was frightened, terrified in fact, so terrified with horror that I could fall by her side and wait. Wait for someone to get us, but I didn't. I ran. The thought of getting caught, ran over in my mind so many times, I was confused about what was reality or not.

I was half a footstep away from my crime. I thought, if I go I will have the guilt forever, so I turned, stopped and looked around. All of those people with smiles, happiness, no guilt, just something in their memories.

Nothing was as bad as the feeling of a black-hearted, middle-aged murderer, but I couldn't stand it. I ran, tripped, but carried on. A bad thing was coming, but I didn't care. I was running out of breath. I couldn't believe it. It wasn't my fault, I'd had arguments with everyone I knew, even myself. But I didn't know if she'd be there. I didn't know if my mother had gone yet, but I carried on.

Inside the house was the body of my friend who had been lying there for hours. I didn't know what my mother would say, but there behind me she was standing, waiting for an answer . . . a reason why?

Seth Elton (11)
North Bridge House School

A DAY IN THE LIFE OF AN ARTIST

A day in the life of an artist would be like having your own world and universe. Everything you see is your own image of a good lifestyle. Everything you see would be transformed into a picture of peace and war.

The word 'art' keeps echoing in your mind as if your life depends on it. from day to day, you think how fast the real world is moving on, but in your life it would be happy and sad at the same time, moving on slowly. To some people, paintings look weird, but to the artist, it is letting all your thoughts onto paper.

Paintings calm you down and never give you nervous points. Your room is filled with thoughts, paintbrushes, pencils and paper. Sometimes a painting starts with an easy thought and a dream with care.

Sometimes you get so involved that no one can interfere with one object. When you are talking about art, you even start a whole new language. No one ever knows your deep secrets and feelings, which is one good thing, because no matter what, your mouth is zipped up as if you have no voice.

Olga Formalnova (10)
North Bridge House School

SPOOK HOUSE

Tanya woke up just in time to see her sister Petra faint. She leapt out of bed and shook her. There was no reply. Horrified, she ran to the kitchen and grabbed a bottle of water, then ran back to her room. The water gushed out onto Petra's head and she woke up with a start, breathing heavily.
'What happened?' questioned Tanya.
'I . . . I saw a spectre, a ghost,' gasped Petra.
'You're joking!' said Tanya, gaping.
'Nope,' said Petra, shaking her head.

At that moment, a door creaked open, then slammed shut and locked itself. The same happened to all the windows in the room. Then, at that moment, a spine-chilling howl was let out. The girls shrieked, but then Tanya bravely said, 'What do you want and who are you?'
'I have come to take you to Hell. I am your worst nightmare,' a cracked voice hissed.
But Tanya wasn't too scared. She ran over to a curtain and was just going to open it when icy-cold hands pulled her back and threw her across the room. She felt in her pocket and switched on the torch, thrusting it in the ghost's face. 'Mission accomplished!' she whispered.

Juliet McNelly (11)
North Bridge House School

SHE SCREAMS

One day, my next door neighbour screamed. I ran over to her house and said, 'What's the matter?'
She said, 'I . . . I saw a . . . a ghost!' She was choked with terror.

That night, she couldn't go to sleep. She told herself that demons and monsters were rubbish. She said, 'I'm not afraid anymore.'

After that had happened, two nights later, all the demons, ghouls and monsters came crawling from underneath her bed. She was still asleep all night, until sunrise. All the monsters, demons and ghouls went away. The Evil One said they were not real, but one night, something came along.

It was pitch-black, she got scared. Suddenly she heard a creaking sound. She heard footsteps, they sounded squidgy and slimy. When she turned the light on, she saw a hideous, freak-show creature. She screamed so loudly, all the lights from nearly every house went on. She carried on screaming. The hideous monster grabbed her and she kicked him straight away and ran as fast as she could . . . but he ran faster and grabbed and bit.

Jonathan Fernandes (10)
North Bridge House School

THE LOVE THAT WORKS OUT

There was once a man named Jason who loved a woman called Yvonne. Jason loved her but she had a husband. Jason could do nothing about that, so he told her he loved her.
She said, 'I can't.'
'But why not?' said Jason.
'Because . . . because he will kill me, that husband of mine!'
'Well, I will put him in hospital! I will come round your house and fight him and if I die, I die.'
'OK!' said Yvonne.

So that night Jason went to Yvonne's house and had the fight. The fight went like this . . . Jason punched Yvonne's husband Simon in the face and then Simon got a knife out and stabbed Jason. Yvonne called 999 and an ambulance came.

The next morning Jason woke up and he and Yvonne got a priest and they married. A week later Jason came out of hospital, then later in the year they had kids and they lived happily ever after.

Conor O'Sullivan (9)
St Agnes RC Primary School, Barnet

I'M A WITCH!

One day at school I was practising a new spell and accidentally made myself and Maddy, my friend, 1cm tall. We tried to get our teacher's attention but Mr Craft didn't see us, so we climbed up to him by using the books on his table as stairs.

Finally we reached him and crawled onto his tie. We managed to climb up to his ear and called to Mr Craft for help, but he could not hear us. Maddy slipped and we both fell into Mr Craft's ear. We started climbing but we had gone too far and we found ourselves in his brain! It was so soggy and slippery.

We found Mr Craft's eyes. We needed help, so I got my book of magic out and found a spell to make him obey my commands. I got him to go out of the school. We eventually got him to my house and made him tell my parents what had happened. He was talking like a robot! Soon after they got us out of Mr Craft's head and I undid the shrinking spell. Poor Mr Craft, he didn't know why he was there or how he got there.

Megan Abbott (9)
St Agnes RC Primary School, Barnet

THE CHASE

Running, running away from demons, hungry demons that have everlasting energy, that once they've finished one victim, they go on to the next. I'm not sure how I got here, in the demon world, but one thing's for sure, if I stop running I'll get eaten alive.

I'm looking around and all I see is red ground, otherwise nothing. A demon came so close that I could feel his breath, then my legs were moving so fast that they were just a blur. I looked as far as I could and I could see a big, black hole, a hole that didn't have a bottom. So I headed for it, hoping I could do a quick turn and lead them into it. But as I pick up speed, it is getting harder for me to turn. I am getting closer and it is getting harder to control my movements. I am so close that even the demons have turned away and eh . . . 'Ahhhh!'

Then I woke up.

Perry Tobin-Stevens (9)
St Scholastica's RC Primary School, Hackney

Monster Munch

I was woken by a shocking *smash*. I asked myself, should I go and see or not? I decided to go and see what it was.

I was half-way down the stairs, when I heard a smash from the living room. I thought whatever it was, it moves fast. Then I couldn't be bothered to walk down the stairs, I flung myself over the banisters, *thump!*

I was trembling, I didn't know why. I was trying to find a horrible something. I got to see the mysterious thing and it was an ugly monster. I stumbled into a bedroom and saw it was stuck behind the TV eating everything around it.

I thought, should I move the TV? What will happen if I do and what will happen if I don't? I knew whatever I did, I'd regret it. I decided to move the TV thinking whatever happened, I wouldn't care. I moved the TV and suddenly it shot at me. I fell on the floor scrambling away. I got up and saw it had knocked the answerphone on the floor.

It started beeping, louder and louder, until . . . it was my alarm clock beeping.

Ben Slade (9)
St Scholastica's RC Primary School, Hackney

WEREWOLF FEVER

It was a stuffy night and Rachel woke up. Beads of sweat dripped down her. She looked at her wristwatch. 2:00, it read. Rachel decided to go for a walk. She took off her dotty nightdress and put on some green shorts and a bright orange top. She slipped on her trainers and grabbed a torch so she could see. She didn't want to wake her parents, so she pulled up her window and leaned out. 'Bullseye!' she exclaimed. She was on the first floor, so she could easily jump out. She stuffed her torch in her pocket and slid out of her window. She yanked out her torch and flicked it on.

Suddenly, she heard something panting behind her. She spun round, but the noise had stopped. She plodded down the street and when she got to Fountain road, she heard it again. She ran for her life. Then she came face to face with it. Wolf, she thought. Werewolf. She ran into the woods and up a tree. I'm safe, she thought, but the werewolf was there, licking its paws . . .

Dana McCusker (9)
St Scholastica's RC Primary School, Hackney

THE MYSTERIOUS ADVENTURE

One sunny day, I woke up and had a message on my pager. It said, 'Come to the supermarket, then we will go on an adventure. We will go to Disneyland, Paris!'

I went to the supermarket and went on the adventure I was promised. When we got there, we saw Mickey Mouse and he said, 'Hello, do you want to go on a ride?'
We said, 'Yes, please!'
We went on a ride and it was a roller coaster. When we got off, we felt sick.
Goofy said, 'Do you want me to show you around Disneyland?'
We said, 'Yes, please.' He showed us round Disneyland and he showed us all the rides, all the funfairs and when he had finished showing us around, we went on one of the rides.

After, we went home and had a cup of tea, then we went to bed.

Kevin Kotey (9)
St Scholastica's RC Primary School, Hackney

THE SUMARI GANG ADVENTURER

A group of friends, the Samaria Gang, were invited to Junayde's birthday party. The gang members were Ash, Junayde, Mathias and Gavin.

They missed the bus, but managed to shop rapidly for an hour. Then Gavin threw one of his doubled cards away. *Suddenly, a world of purple appeared!* Everyone was excited. Only the gang and a serious looking, weird man with golden hair and bulky muscles remained. He shouted, 'Kamahamahaaa.' A blinding flash appeared from his palm. Everyone was stunned. Junayde and I jumped out of the way as the light beam hit them and they turned to stone. I accidentally hit a bag that contained a fake sword, trying anything to beat him. Suddenly, the rubber sword became solid.

I showed Junayde the sword and we made a plan. Junayde viciously clung onto the man's back while I tried to stab him. He flung Junayde off like a feather. I tried to cut him in half but he stopped the sword. I pushed the sword with all my might, but it would not work. Junayde helped me to push the sword into the man and we cut him in half. Suddenly, the world glowed blue and returned to normal. The gang decided to keep it all a secret.

Meanwhile, Gavin and Mathias returned to normal and we lived happily ever after.

Jean-Claude Isaie (9)
St Scholastica's RC Primary School, Hackney

OFF TO FUTURE, BACK TO PRESENT

One cold night in October, our cousin Rebecca decided to stay in our aunty's house. We played Hallowe'en games. My aunty's house is very old, she keeps her private belongings in one room, in a safe.

After we went to bed, Rebecca thought everyone was sleeping. She got up and went to the secret room. She stuck her head in the safe, she was in the future.

Rebecca landed in a big city called Atlantis II. There were glass tunnels that cars went through, people were dressed in shiny clothes. All the things were modern.

She liked this place, but wanted to go home. She found a dream room and decided to wish for her family and she got her family back. She was safe at home. She said to herself, the present is better than the future.

Hannah Phillips (9)
St Scholastica's RC Primary School, Hackney

Renting Videos Can Be Murder

Jason and Kate rented an Itchy and Scratchy movie because like everyone, they love The Simpsons. A girl named Kate Kerting and her best friend, Jason Jackson, met at 56 Fearing Road. Fortunately and very conveniently, Blockbusters was just down the road. Are the movies scary, you ask. The best there are, in fact. Especially the Itchy and Scratchy selection. OK, time to go on. Are you sure you want to read on? Here goes.

It was a scorching summer's day. Kate shouted, 'Come on, we don't have all day. Do you want to rent that video of Itchy and Scratchy?' 'I'm coming!' Jason hollered.

She pulled open the old, creaky door that led to the eye-goggling selection of Itchy and Scratchy movies. They had seen every one, except the last and, would you believe it . . . it was the last one there. They practically flew to the counter. They rushed to Kate's house and dived to the video recorder and pummelled the switch on the TV.
'What!' Jason howled. 'Oooooh nooooo!'

What happened to them?

Jade Smith (9)
St Scholastica's RC Primary School, Hackney

ON A DARK NIGHT

One dark and stormy night, everyone was in bed. I woke up tired after a bad dream. I was thirsty, so I made my way downstairs, but on the way I noticed blood on the stairs and the walls. Footprints that were not human. At this point, I was getting worried. All the kitchen knives were gone. Suddenly, I saw a hand with one of the kitchen knives. Step by step, it got closer. All of a sudden, everything went *blank!* I woke up on the kitchen floor. It was all a dream, *or was it?*

I looked in the bathroom mirror and I was as pale as a sheet. I could not believe my eyes, I was a ghost! How I wished it was a dream. I closed my eyes and wished it hadn't happened. Facing reality, I'd be a ghost forever now, and I couldn't do anything about it. Suddenly, I saw a pale-looking girl. She was a ghost too.
'Who are you?'
'You can see me, you must be a spirit too.'
'Ghost, you mean.'
'I prefer spirit, if you don't mind.'
'Oh, I see.'
From then, we were best friends. She taught me how to float things around and how to fly.
'You know what? I'm glad I'm a ghost.'
'Spirit.'
'Oh yeah!'

Charlotte Dunne (9)
St Scholastica's RC Primary School, Hackney

THE ROAD TO MOUNT HORROR

One day, there was a boy named Charlie who was going to spend a month at his aunty's house. He packed his bag and gladly exclaimed, 'That's it, ready to go.'
His mother drove him to the west of England and his aunt was waiting for him with an interesting smile on her face.

Since he had been there many times before, he had a friend named Sally, a senior to him. The next morning, he had been commanded to be taken to the school. Sally, obeying Aunt Susie's order, took him to the school in the cloudy mountains. Old Fork School.

As soon as they came home, since Charlie wanted to be a photographer, he went into the woods to take some snapshots at night. They were out until at least full moon, then Sally made a great suggestion, to go to school. They went there, into the dark hallway, tightly grasping their torch. Suddenly, the great door closed behind them.

Zombies and devils passed them and Sally and Charlie exchanged glances. A wizard suddenly cast a spell which caused them to burn to ashes.

Franklyn Addo Koroma (8)
St Scholastica's RC Primary School, Hackney

INVISIBILITY

'Ahhh, kill it!' Jack said, screaming.
'It's only a crab,' Mum said.
Jack ran around madly, but then the doorbell rang. 'Who can that be?' Jack said. 'Hi, guys.'
'Hi Jack, Mr Procopules' made a new invention, an invisibility ray. Let's go!'

Once they got there, Jack said, 'Hi Mr Procopules, what happened?'
'The invisibility ray is broken, stand back!' he shouted.

Crash, bang, rumble!

'Aha, it works!' Mr Procopules exclaimed.
'Is that all you can think of? We're invisible,' Jack exclaimed.
'Come back in six weeks for the cure,' Mr Procopules said.

Six weeks later, the boys came for the cure.
'Drink this,' Mr Procopules said.
'What's wrong with you? This has turned us into donkeys!'
'Oops!'

Toby Osei-Baffour (9)
St Scholastica's RC Primary School, Hackney

BACK IN TIME

One cold night I went to bed at midnight as usual, then in the morning, I was in a different dimension. I was looking around and found the bone of a dinosaur's head. Suddenly, it started to move. When it had stopped raining, I went to see the bones but they had disappeared.

I was running till I saw a diplodocus. It was not moving, but it was still alive. Suddenly, I was running for my life because the diplodocus was trying to eat me.

A stegosaurus was waiting and I thought he was waiting for me, so I jumped on its back and I hit it, then it started running.

I saw a tomb, so I jumped into it, but it was scary because it started to shake, then I saw a T-rex. I ran and suddenly, I fell through a hole and I was back in my room.

Roar! I found a T-rex with his jaws open. He pounced and gobbled me up!

Euan McIntyre (9)
St Scholastica's RC Primary School, Hackney

SEF DID IT

In the countryside of Scotland, where the tall trees tower like skyscrapers, on a hill stood a mysterious boarding school.

In the school a fight was taking place in a dormitory of four boys. The boys were Ron, a plump boy with blond hair and a nose the size of two lemons, and Sef, a tall generous boy with brown bulging eyes.

Suddenly the head teacher, Mrs Crump, came in . . .

'Stop that this instant or else!' she exclaimed.
They stopped straight away as if they were hypnotised. 'Yes Miss,' Ron and Sef croaked as Mrs Crump left.

'I'll kill you, you just wait,' Sef threatened Ron.

The following week at dinner Ron went to the toilet. Sef followed him and soon came back, but Ron didn't. Jack noticed some red goo on Sef's hand, but Sef wiped it off so he couldn't see it anymore.

Later that day a voice screamed from the toilet.

Everybody rushed down to the toilets where they found Bill standing in front of Ron's dead body.

Everybody thought Sef had killed Ron since he threatened him and came to dinner with red goo on his hand, but then that night the boys went to Mrs Crump's office to ask about the murder. From down the corridor they heard Mrs Crump say, *'Great,* I killed Ron, now who to kill next!'

Jacob Crofts (10)
St Stephen's CE Primary School

WHO DID IT?

The phone rang shrilly through my silent office. I picked up the receiver. 'Hello, Special Detective Maysun speaking,' I answered.

'Hi Maysun, it's Uncle Mickieth. I've got a mission for you. You'll also have a partner called Sadia Hoque, but you'll have to be careful with her, she is a grumpy type of girl,' he chuckled.

My mission was to find out who had murdered Dr Wilkins. I arrived at the clinic straight away. I couldn't believe my eyes when I saw Dr Wilkins' dead body.

That's where I started my investigation. I took some photographs and went back to my office where I met my new partner, Sadia Hoque. Uncle was right, she was a grumpy sort of girl!

I showed her the photographs and told her to go and put them in a red file in my locker. I gave her the number: 623321.

The next day we arrived at the clinic. We picked up the knife and took fingerprints from it. Soon we were back at the office. I told Sadia to put the new clues in my locker.

Two days later, I decided to go back through the clues. I went to my locker and dialled in the number. I took out the red folder and to my horror the clues were gone!

At that very moment a phone call came, it was Uncle.

'Hello Maysun, I wanted to tell you something . . . Sadia is the murderer!'

Maysun Hoque (10)
St Stephen's CE Primary School

SPOOKS

One moody morning Miss Jackson, our teacher, announced that we would be studying history. I was doomed; I had forgotten my history homework. The new boy in our class was called Devirel Potter. He had something spooky in his eyes, they were as red as blood. Last month I asked him what happened to his eyes and suddenly my eyes went dizzy, then he disappeared. I knew something strange was going on.

The funny thing was that nobody noticed him. When they were doing the register they did not say his name for some reason. That lesson, Miss Jackson allowed me to take the register down. On my way down I saw Devirel and his mates hanging around because they were in trouble. They started to boss me around and threw me to the ground. Suddenly Devirel's eyes gleamed, rolled to the back of his head and then came back. When I turned around, Miss Jackson was standing there. I felt really relieved and then she began to scream loudly. She was melting! I could not believe it. I heard her shout: 'Close the curtains!' and realised she was a vampire.

Dysney Cline-Decker (10)
St Stephen's CE Primary School

THE UNREMOVABLE FACE

'I'm dying, I'm dying . . . ' echoed a voice from the kitchen.

What was that noise, thought Mr Greck. He was tall and had a round face and freckles. He went to open the door. He placed his hand onteh cold handle and opened it like a gentle breeze gliding through the night sky.

In front of him was . . . nothing!

He was relieved to see nothing there and he gladly went back to watching the TV.

A week later he noticed something sticking out of the kitchen floor. He thought it was the pattern of a face. It was pale yellow and his wrinkly skin and a big cut from one side of the face to the other.

The next day, he told the housekeeper about the face in the floor. She tried, but could not remove it. At last they decided to give up and call the police. The police pulled up the concrete floor and they found a skeleton. They told Mr Greck he was living on top of a graveyard. When they uncovered the head, it was . . . *fresh!* The face yelled, 'Leave us in peace!'

Yasmin Abdi (9)
St Stephen's CE Primary School

WHERE DREAMS TURN INTO NIGHTMARES

Sara was asleep, dreaming, you could say. She was quite a dreamer when it came to dreaming.

'Would you like some candyfloss, Princess Candy?' cooed a multicoloured nightingale.
'Yes please. And make sure that there are lots of chocolate sprinkles on it!' And off the nightingale flew, taking out Princess Candy's orders.
'Ah, this is the life!' Sara sighed, swinging on the hammock, drinking a cup of tropical juice.

'*Shriek!*' Suddenly, all the peaceful silence was interrupted by a disturbing tearing sound. Sara woke up with a start. There, right in front of her eyes was a door. Around it, it glowed, like it was begging to be opened.

'No, don't!' Sara screamed. A force pulled her to the door; her hand was already turning the door knob and it opened. A land loomed ahead. There were few lights and it seemed deserted. She wobbled on the thin piece of wood separating her from the deserted land.

'Nooo!' Sara dropped into the forbidden land and the door shut and disappeared. This was her punishment for dreaming about big things. Sara now haunts people who do the same thing as her, so watch out!

Rachel Koramoah (9)
Stroud Green Primary School

NIGHTMARES

It was Saturday, a really hot Saturday. The Tilt family were sitting down on a bench in the park, while their youngest daughter, Claire, was sleeping. This was her dream.

Claire was in an unknown world, where everything was huge, and Claire was very small. Suddenly, she stepped in a foot chain trap. She screamed loudly 'Help me . . . please!'

Immediately a middle sized old woman came and said in a crinkled old voice, 'I will help you.'
'You'd better,' Claire said pushily.

Suddenly, the nice old lady offering to help Claire turned into a monster, a green ogre with an axe dripping blood.

'I will get you!' it bellowed in a huge voice. Claire woke up.
'Argghh!' she screamed. Her parents tried to calm her down, but that did not work. They went home. *It was a . . . nightmare!*

'Bedtime!' shouted Mrs Tilt from downstairs. Claire was reading a story. As soon as Claire switched off the light, she saw a figure and it said, 'I'll get you!'

Denisha Koramoah (8)
Stroud Green Primary School

TONGUE TWISTER POEM

One wicked witch
Two tired, tortured trolls
Three threatening tigers
Four fragil flowers
Five fluffy flies
Six slithering snakes
Seven sick sparrows
Eight annoying elephants
Nine nasty newts
Ten talented trampolines
Eleven evil enemies
Twelve tiny toddlers
Thirteen thin trees
Fourteen flat feet
Fifteen frightened fish
Sixteen stupid squirrels
Seventeen skinny seals
Eighteen eager eels
Nineteen nosey nurses
Twenty tough tangles
Twenty-one tempered teams
Twenty-two tricky triplets
Twenty-three tasty tunas
Twenty-four tender turnips
Twenty-five teenager trimmers
Twenty-six terrific tournaments
Twenty-seven tragic traders
Twenty-eight timid tramps
Twenty-nine terrible things
Thirty thick thorns
Thirty-one tall temples
Thirty-two terrifying tales
Thirty-three total tasks
Thirty-four troubling traffic
Thirty-five truthful teachers

Thirty-six tight ties
Thirty-seven talking tarantulas
Thirty-eight tired trash
Thirty-nine nude nuts
Forty fruity flavours
Forty-one fabulous forks
Forty-two fantastic factories
Forty-three fictitious fashion
Forty-four fake flags
Forty-five fluffy flamingoes
Forty-six former formulas
Forty-seven forever friends
Forty-eight ferocious falls
Forty-nine filthy flats
Fifty fine furnisher
Fifty-one fair females
Fifty-two flaxen faces
Fifty-three fanciful fairies
Fifty-four far families
Fifty-five future favours
Fifty-six funny fields.

Chinyere Nwimo Ogu (9)
Stroud Green Primary School

A DAY IN THE LIFE OF AN ANT

Once there lived a family of ants. There was Mother, Father and the smallest called Toby. Toby had a friend called Wormy and they always had great times together.

One day while Toby was playing, he heard gigantic footsteps coming. It was the man who owned the house. Toby was frightened. He scuttled in and told his mum, 'You're pulling my legs aren't you?' She didn't believe him. He went to tell Wormy, he was sure he'd believe him.
Wormy was petrified, 'Oh no, we're all going to die,' he whispered cautiously.
'No, we are going to save you and my family.' Just then it started raining, the man went indoors.

Next day Toby went to pick crumbs from the garden for breakfast. The next thing he knew he was in a box with Wormy, they had been kidnapped by the little girl. They managed to escape from a hole in the wall that led them to a mouse's hole. Toby asked for help but it was the wrong way out. They found themselves in the kitchen. Now the girl had found them and was chasing them through the house. Out through the cat flap and into the garden. Toby called a tiny taxi to take them home. Wormy moved in with them.

Now the family are in a much safer place and shelter from the rain. Can you guess where? I'll leave that to you.

Aliya Fenghour (9)
Summerside Primary School

THE RING

One stormy night when I was on my way home from work, my car seemed to conk out on me. It would be the one day I didn't have my mobile phone on me, but in the distance I saw a house where hopefully I might be able to phone from.

I wandered towards the house and knocked on the door. After a little while, an old lady opened it. 'How may I help you?' she sniggered.
'Can I use your phone please? My car has broken down.' I asked.
'Yes,' she replied.

Whilst I was using the phone, the line seemed to go dead. I didn't think to tell her, as a ring on the side, a very posh one, distracted me. Maybe, I thought to myself, I could steal it and give it to my wife as I had forgotten that it was our anniversary.

Later that night, I went to where the lady was sleeping. I got a very sharp knife and chopped her finger off.

The following year, my car broke down again at the same place (funnily enough) where it had broken down last year. I was dreading going back to the house in the distance, but I had to go. I carefully knocked on the door. The same old lady opened up. 'Hello, can I use your phone please, and who did that to your finger?' I cackled sarcastically.
She then suddenly jumped at me and screamed, *'It was you!'*

Naeem Mitha (10)
William Davies Primary School

THE AUSTIN SEVEN

I wouldn't have ended up in this wheelchair if I hadn't had that serious car crash. I don't remember that much of it, though I used to have such good memories. Do you want to hear about it?

Stacey and I were married and we had a blue Bedford van. It was quite rotten, though I say it myself, it was a good car. Stacey was getting fed up with the van because it was very old. She asked me to get a new and modern car. I had to agree with her.

The next morning, I rushed to the shops and bought the Loot newspaper. Whilst I was walking home, there on the bottom right hand corner in big bold writing it said 'Austin Seven for £900, modern'. Just then, I brightened up a bit. I told Stacey, but she didn't want it. She thought there was something strange about it. that night I phoned up for the Austin Seven and they said I could go and have a look at it the next day at 9:35.

The next morning, I ate my breakfast as quickly as I could and rushed to see the brand new car. The man was very old and he had a broken leg.
'I'm in this wheelchair for the rest of my life,' he said, in a sweet voice. Then he asked, 'Is your name Edward?'
I replied, 'It certainly is. How did you know?'
He never answered back.

The car was as good as gold and never even had one scratch on it. The windows were nice and sparkly and the inside was just perfect. It was just the car I had been looking for. I gave the man the money and walked home with a big grin on my face, but just then I had second thoughts about how I was going to tell Stacey. I knew she wouldn't like it.

I led her through to the Austin Seven . . .

Asma Patel (11)
William Davies Primary School

THE KING AND THREE DAUGHTERS

A king and his three daughters lived in a large castle with doors made of gold. One day, the king asked his daughters to describe how they loved him.

The first one said, 'Father, I love you as much as gold and silver.'
The second one said, 'Father, I love you as much as the sun and moon.'
Finally, the last one said, 'Father, I love you as much as sugar.'

The king went red and ordered the young girl to leave his palace. The princess did as she was told. Years passed and the girl married a prince. This prince one day decided to invite his wife's father for a meal. When the princess heard this,, she commanded her servants that whatever they were going to cook, not to add any sugar to it as she knew her father would not be pleased.

At last the old king arrived, bringing many presents. When the time came for the meal, the king ate the starter and main course joyfully, but when he took a bite from the chocolate cake, his face went a funny shape and he spat it out.
'For heaven's sake, what is this?' he questioned.
'Father, this is the cake without any sugar. Don't you remember, years ago I told you I loved you as much as sugar and you sent me out? Well, I left and bravely found a lovely home, and knowing you were coming, I did not add sugar to your food, remembering what happened,' recited the princess calmly.

The king felt very ashamed and asked for forgiveness from his daughter.

Nabilah Sannan (10)
William Davies Primary School

THE TOOTH FAIRIES

All of the tooth fairies were gathered at the top of the tooth castle waiting for the tooth queen's approval to set off. 'You may now be off,' announced the queen. Lucy and Laura set off together - they were the best of friends, they went everywhere together. They flew over clouds, meadows and fields.

They finally arrived at Rebecca's house, she had just had her first tooth. The house looked like a small cottage with red, flowery curtains. Lucy and Laura went all the way around the house looking for Rebecca's bedroom window. The window was slightly ajar. Laura flew in first. She noticed that Rebecca was a girly-girl - she had pinkish wallpaper, a play dressing table and thousands of Barbie dolls. Lucy attempted to fly in, but she wouldn't fit all of the way through. 'You've been scoffing too many chocolates!' complained Laura. Laura pulled and pulled. 'Be careful, you don't want to scatter the sleep dust,' she whispered, being careful not to wake Rebecca up.

The window was too big and heavy for Laura to lift open. Lucy remembered the cat flap they had passed. 'Wait, do you remember that cat flap we passed? We can go through there,' she suggested.
Laura agreed. She flew back out.

But then, disaster struck. Lucy accidentally dropped the coin and it made a huge noise, which woke up the cat. The cat snarled and chased the fairies up the stairs. 'Quick! Sprinkle some sleep dust on him!' ordered Laura.
Lucy grabbed some sleep dust and sprinkled it over the cat. The cat went to sleep with an enormous yawn. Lucy went and got the coin from the bottom of the stairs.
'Don't worry, he's asleep,' said Laura with a sigh of relief.
Laura and Lucy wanted to get out of there as soon as possible. They hurried along to Rebecca's room. Laura gently put the coin on Rebecca's bedside drawer. As they wanted to get out of there as soon as possible, they went through the catflap, being very careful not to wake the cat. While Laura and Lucy were flying back to the tooth castle, Laura asked, 'Why did we have so much trouble on this journey?'
'Dunno.'

Laura and Lucy arrived at the tooth castle.
'So how was your journey?' questioned the tooth queen.
'It was OK. One of the best,' replied Lucy.
'Good, so where's the tooth?' queried the queen.
'Uh oh.'

Neelam Samplay (11)
William Davies Primary School

Do Computers Talk?

'Bye, Steve!' shouted Thomas, waving his bony fingers in the freezing air. Thomas stepped into his house and was taking off his wet, muddy shoes that had turned from white to a mouldy brown colour. As he bent down to put his shoes on the shoe rack, he noticed by the mat was a mousetrap with a bit of custard-coloured cheese at the end of it.

Thomas decided to ignore the mousetrap as Mum had probably put it there, just in case a mouse came into the sitting room. But as Thomas went up the stairs, he saw more and more strange changes! Thomas dragged his feet into his bedroom that was covered with amazing posters of his best football players, hoping it would be as sparkling as he had left it in the morning, but was it though?

Thomas rushed into his bedroom with his eyes shut tight. He quickly opened his eyes with an enormous grin on his face, but as he looked around the room, his smile faded away and his heart sank. His cupboard was left in a dump with clothes scattered on the floor, overlapping and forming a rainbow. His screwed-up magazines were all divided in each corner of the room and his brand new computer game (Red Alert), which was sparkling because he had been cleaning it every time he played it, had long scratches on it. Let alone that it was broken into a million pieces among the rainbow of clothes.

Thomas pounded down the stairs, slamming doors on his way. As he reached the kitchen, he heard Mum humming to an unknown song.
'Mum, what has Sporty done to my room? She's broken my CD, the most expensive one you bought me!' exploded Thomas, his face reaching boiling point.
'Calm down, honey, and stop blaming Sporty. Gran came round today and decided to take Sporty out for a day as she was alone at home and fed up!' explained Mum, putting the mouth-watering fish fingers and chips in the oven.
'But Mum . . .' moaned Thomas, throwing himself onto the wooden chair.
'Go to your room and calm down, right now!' snapped Mum, pointing her fat finger at Thomas.

He dragged his feet out of the kitchen with his eyes burning and filled with water. He decided to go on the computer to calm him down a little. He switched the computer on countless times, but it didn't work. Thomas decided that this was his very last attempt. This time it worked, instead of a bright blue screen with a gentle sound, a grey coloured screen appeared with an old lady's crinkled face gazing at him, with her ginger coloured eyes wide open. She gave an evil smile and whispered, 'Come by my side, little boy, I won't harm you. Come on.'

Thomas' heart started to beat fast, as he clenched his fist. He gulped with such a fright as all of a sudden, the room turned as dark as space. Before he even opened his mouth to speak, someone from somewhere poked their enormous fingers with sharp, pointy nails at him, grabbed hold of his face and at that very moment, his whole body swished through and . . .

Pooja Bharucha (11)
William Davies Primary School

A Smashing Sleep-Over!

'Oh, wow!' exclaimed Gemma. 'This is nothing like that boring old clubhouse! It's definitely had a fabulous make-over!'

That was true. I had bright and glittery material for the curtains - reds, oranges and yellows, three purple beanbags and a great feast on the pine table in the middle of the room. All kinds of food; chips, cake, drinks and chocolate. There was also a collection of videos, CDs and other stuff near the stereo, TV and video.

'What shall we do first?' questioned Amy.
'Let's watch the movie we rented out and stuff our faces too. I think Mum's got a surprise, I'll just go over and check,' I answered.
Leaving them shocked, I ran into the kitchen and brought out the three delicious home made chocolate ice cream sundaes. 'Here we are! Three scrumptious chocolate sundaes.'
I inserted the video; we all changed into our pyjamas and snuggled up in our sleeping bags with the food.

'That was fantastic - I loved the part where she got her clothes trapped in the car and she got dragged all the way until they reached the motorway,' I laughed.
'I'm feeling quite tired now - I think we should go to sleep. Tomorrow we can have a make-up session and order some pizza!' Amy suggested.
They all nodded. I went to draw the curtains and lock the door.

The next morning, we all woke up at 10 o'clock. We were probably exhausted from staying up all night. Mum came in to see if we wanted breakfast. 'No, we'll just stick to what was left from last night, Mrs Smith,' explained Gemma.
'Okay, I'll be upstairs if you need me.'

The make-up session was great, but then the phone rang and I think Mum answered it because a few minutes later, she came running down the stairs and out into the garden. 'Girls, Gemma's mum needs to go to hospital for her appointment. She forgot all about it, so she's going to come and pick Gemma and Amy up now,' said Mum, sympathetically.

As Mum left the room, we gave each other disappointed looks.
'Hey, it doesn't matter. We can have another one, maybe when your mum's more organised?' suggested Amy politely.
Both of us nodded. 'We should tidy up,' I said. We all agreed, it was a *smashing sleep-over!*

Salma Zannath (11)
William Davies Primary School

HITCH-HIKER

Jane as on her way home from the dark, misty field where she had been camping. She had tons of baggage, so she thought she should hitch-hike, as there was no bus or train.

She waited for ages and finally a flash red Porsche came along. She put her cold, shivering thumb up as her silky blonde hair whistled in the icy wind. She was desperate to get home. Jane could see clearly through her dark blue eyes that it was a man, he didn't look like he was going to stop or slow down.

As she entered the car she could see he was in his mid-thirties with dark ginger hair like a lion's mane on fire. He gave a cheesy grin that made Jane glow. His dark green eyes made Jane glow, his dark green eyes made her spine shiver.

'Not exactly travelling first class are you?' he said looking down at her muddy shoes. She forced a smile to her a face. 'Where to love?' he said with a strong cockney accent.

'Home please,' she replied.
'And where is that?' he said with a grin.
'Straight ahead,' she said with her smooth red lips.

The journey was going smoothly until the driver asked her name.
'Jane,' she replied softly, 'and your's?' she said curiously.
'Alfred. But my friends call me Al,' he was getting louder. 'Don't you ever get scared hitch-hiking?' he said sounding intrigued.
'No, not really. I don't like hitch-hiking very often,' she replied starting to shiver.
'Did you see the thing in the Oxford Gazette about the murder?' he said quietly.

A burst of fear went through her mind. Who was this man? she thought, he could be a murderer or anything.

'Don't you get scared that a driver will come out with a giant knife and stab you?' he said cautiously.
'There are not that sort ofpeople around here,' she said not believing herself.

'Are you sure?' he said getting creepier by the minute.

Al went on about the death in Oxford for ages.

'So if *I had a knife you wouldn't be sacred? Not that I do!*' he said with a crafty grin that hadn't moved from his face throughout the journey.
'Jus . . . just drop me off here,' Jane quickly replied with a large stutter.

Jane was as terrified as a dormouse being chased by a ten-foot elephant. It was as if the road was caving in on them, there was complete silence apart from the odd crackle of the engine. Crkkk, there was one final crackle and the car stopped.

'You sure you don't want me to take you down the road Darlin'?' he said as his eyes sparkled in the moonlight.
'Ye . . . yes I'm sure,' she said while she shivered.

She picked up her baggage with her quivering fingers and dragged them out of the car. Jane started walking down the dark gloomy lane. All she could hear was the clanging of her tight muddy shoes on the gravel, in her mind she could still hear all the things that Alfred had said. She had never been so terrified in her life, she rushed homewards.

That night when she was in her bed she slept like a log, apart from the uncontrollable nightmares. Al or Alfred had *not* just stopped at the crossroads, he had followed Jane all the way home with *killing* in mind. The door had been locked so he crept up to the window. He saw her sweet face. 'Beautiful,' he muttered. He put his head through first. After a split second the whole window and frame came crashing down onto his head. After a minute his ginger hair flowed red, as Jane slept on unaware of the tragedy.

She spent the rest of her life in jail accused of a crime that puzzled everyone.

Archie Backhouse (11) & Zed Callaghan (10)
William Patten Primary School

JETHRO AND CALVERT'S ADVENTURES

Egypt

4009BC - The mummy lay in darkness. When the hinges of the door creaked open people in black cloaks burst in. They grabbed his treasure. They ran out and slammed the door. The mummy got angry. He wanted revenge.

2005AD

'I can't believe we have to go on the plane by ourselves,' Jethro said.
'Well, at least we get to see your uncle,' said Calvert.

Jethro and Calvert were at the airport to go to Spain. Their mums and dads had said that as soon as they got there they would see Jethro's uncle. They said goodbye to their mums and dads and went on the plane. They took their seats and looked around, there was nobody there.

'The plane is about to take off, enjoy your flight.'
'Huh, nobody here,' said Jethro.
'Spain is a popular place, how come nobody wants to come?'

Jethro woke up, the plane had landed.

'Huh, Egypt,' he said.
'I'll race you to that pyramid,' said Calvert.

They raced to the pyramid and *wham!* Jethro fell over a step, flew forward and got a mouthful of sand. While he was spitting it out he saw a step. He climbed down pushing the sand out of the way. Then Calvert's feet tapped across the floor. They opened the door and a horrible scene met their eyes. Before they could run the mummy grabbed them and they fell to the ground. They ran for the door but the mummy had locked it. They ran for the corridor and the mummy didn't see them. Jethro looked at Calvert who had a worried expression on his face.

'What?' said Jethro.
'There's a werewolf behind you. It's almost on you!'
'It's only half an hour until morning, you push him off,' said Jethro.

'Okay,' Calvert replied.

They dodged it for what seemed like hours. Finally it changed and they found a mummy in the sand. Jethro found a book, he picked it up and read the transcription. He read the book. 'Calvert, there's a missing page. I know where it is, it's in the mummy's pocket. I saw it.'

They found him at the museum. Jethro dived and grabbed the page. The mummy saw him across the room. Jethro was in darkness. Calvert slammed beside him. They woke up cornered by mummies in a cold corridor. The mummies unwrapped their bandages. They put the bandages around Jethro and Calvert. Their skin ripped off, all that was left was bone. The pain pierced Jethro's head. They had turned into the mummies and the mummies had turned into them.

They chased the mummies down the corridor, then Jethro fell down a deep hole, Calvert and the mummies close behind. The skin came back and the bandages ripped off. They slammed on the ground.

'Wow, what a wicked dream!'
'That wasn't a dream,' said Calvert.

He showed Jethro the book, its shiny pages were glittering.

Jethro Jenkins (8)
William Patten Primary School

Dangerous Sleeping

Margo's thin wirey legs paced up and down her bedroom as her brunette electric hair swayed from side to side. Her teeth chewed frantically at her bottom lip, day dreaming the whole time! She slowly slipped into bed pulling the duvet cover up to her chin nearly over her head.

Margo's big jade eyes gazed up at the ceiling, a blank smile on her face, she was getting warped into her dream. She was in a moving train. She wasn't dreaming (or that's what she thought). The train was a thin tunnel smelling strongly of burnt electricity, the lights were dim and dusty with dead moths caught in the cases.

'Hello,' she cried as her speech echoed through the pathway to Hell. No reply, then she heard two gruff voices in the distance.

'Jeminaya, get over here with the money!' said the first bandit.

'Yes Bob,' said Jeminaya after a few minutes.

Margo followed the remaining echoes of their voices.

'Hellooooo,' she called again.
'Let's go,' whispered Jeminaya.
'Not yet, remember, hijack,' said Bob.
'Do we have to? I . . . I'm not sure boss, I don't want to.'
'Shut up,' screamed Bob.

Margo was luckily by a phone. She came to her senses, picked up the receiver and dialled 911. She soon got a voice on the other end.

'Hello,' said the cop like he was in a rush.
'Hijack. Quick. 11.04 train,' Margo said like she would save the day!
'Hello,' said the cop again not as rushed as the last time.
'Hello, hello,' cried Margo in a worried tone. No reply.

She flung the receiver back on the hook, forgetting that she could be heard. Jeminaya opened the door flashing his head from side to side.

'Who's there?' he whispered in a slippery voice.
'Come back Jeminaya!' whispered Bob.

A few minutes later Margo opened the door, it creaked! One of the bandits (she couldn't tell which) flung a net over her. Margo got hauled into a small carriage, she and the carriage got coated in parafin.

The heat was unebelievable. She always wanted to know how it felt to be burnt alive, but now, she didn't need to.

Margo's mum walked into Margo's room, lifted the bed covers slowly, and there was her daughter with blisters and scars all over her, burning in nothing but her bed.

Eleanor Sluman (10) & Nat Smith (11)
William Patten Primary School

HEART LOSS

Tears ran down her face as she stared out into the deserted street remembering the death of her father.

The glass smashed as a dark figure flew through the window spreading petrol all over the carpet. She could remember the screams as her father was imbedded in flames. His skin started to shrivel as the fire burnt his flesh into a pile of ash. Sheets of glass stuck out of his body as he made his way to the door. The murderer stopped in front of the doorway blocking the way for the man.

Agony went through her chest as the image appeared in her mind.

The doorbell rang. Sunlight shone through the windows as Betsy walked to the door. When she opened the door she was shocked to find Jonathan standing on the doorstep.

'What are you doing here?'
'Well I was just passing to go to my house.'
'You live in Yorkshire.'
'Fine. I came to see you. There's something I have got to say.' Suddenly he turned his head. 'What the hell happened to your window?'
'Oh, it doesn't matter, so what did you want to say?'
'I'm no good at all that lovey dovey stuff, so I'm just going to say it.'
'Yes.'
'Betsy, I would be honoured if you would be my wife. Your love means everything to me and my soul needs your loving heart to join it in matrimony. Betsy, will you marry me?' he said.

Tears streamed across her cheek as she prepared to speak. 'I . . . will,' she blurted. The wind blew the door in. Leaves were blown frantically around the room. A man with grey trousers and tartan pullover came in. Betsy stepped backwards in disbelief.

'Fa . . . father,' she uttered under her breath, 'is that you?'
'Yes it is. I can only stay for a while but I want you to know that this man is my murderer and you can't marry him!'
'Jonathan . . . is it true?' Betsy asked.
'It was me. I confess. I killed your father.'

The words raced through her mind. She stumbled backwards on the counter and found her hand around the hilt of a kitchen knife. In Jonathan's eyes she could see the knife was poised in mid-air, then she struck. The bloody knife fell to the floor . . . Jonathan let out a scream as he fell onto the cold marble.

Jonathan wanders the street alone and shameful.

Oliver Ings-Williams & Harvey Pegg
William Patten Primary School